GENERAL MacARTHUR

Wisdom and Visions

Compiled by
Edward T. Imparato
COL USAF, (Ret.)

CONTENTS

TURNER
PUBLISHING COMPANY

TURNER PUBLISHING COMPANY

Copyright © 2000 Edward T. Imparato
Publishing Rights: Turner Publishing Company
All Rights reserved.

Designer/Coordinator: Herbert C. Banks II

Library of Congress Control Number: 00-110587

ISBN 978-1-56311-671-1 (hc)
ISBN 978-1-68162-410-5 (pbk)

PREFACE

Why not a book on the Wisdom, Vision and Sayings of General Douglas MacArthur? Was he not one of the great minds in history? Was he not one of the greatest tacticians and strategists in military history? Did he not succeed in great accomplishments in a broad scope of intellectual and practical skills in subjects as wide as the alphabet from A to Z? Was he not the man experts came to talk with in their field of training and knowledge only to come away saying, "He knows more about my profession than I do?" Did he not dazzle with expert knowledge some of the important men in the field of journalism, history, athletics, psychology, politics, government, religion and more?

MacArthur's supremacy as a conversationalist is readily documented. Gene Farmer, experienced and accomplished Senior Editor of *Life* magazine, who had interviewed many of the world's famous men, including Winston Churchill, commented on a conference with MacArthur as follows: "I thought I'd be immune. But something hits you. It's his extraordinary presence. He's Merlin. He casts a spell. I came back and stared at the ceiling of my office all the rest of the day. I had been in the presence of one of the greats."

Col. Armel Dyer, a man of great talent who received his Ph.D. from the University of Oregon in 1968 using the oratory of MacArthur as a vehicle for this honor with his outstanding thesis "The Oratory of General Douglas MacArthur", writes MacArthur at times would read three books a night. MacArthur was well read and in his own memoirs stated he rarely read fiction. MacArthur's power of retention of information read, observed, performed was unbelievably accurate. Only rarely would he miss a minor note. In my research for this work and other MacArthur works in progress, I have read over 300 volumes each having something to say about MacArthur; some of them negative. Never have I heard or read any comment about anyone who had the privilege of visiting with MacArthur face to face come away with a comment other than, "I have just spent an hour with a great man." Even his most vicious critic, a man of great writing talent, but much poor judgement after criticizing MacArthur viciously, ended his discourse with the words, "MacArthur has to rate with the great men of history." Arthur Schlesinger was the critic who simply despised MacArthur never having seen him face to face. Something very typical of all his detractors.

Douglas Southall Freeman, the author of *Lee's Lieutenants* and other great historical works, wrote in a letter to MacArthur that he had such high regard for MacArthur's conduct of his life and military accomplishment that he intended to write a *Lee's Lieutenants* type book on MacArthur.

There is strong evidence, when all the chips are in, all the negatives about MacArthur have been found wanting, all the biographers, historians, analysis of official data and honest to goodness truth seekers, that the final result will be - General Douglas MacArthur was the greatest man who ever lived since the beginning of civilization.

My next work, of a four book series, will cover the accolades received by General MacArthur over his lifetime. At this point in my research and documentation, I have uncovered over 1000 accolades, covering some 600 plus pages. The negatives, with documented proof they are in error, cover one page.

PREAMBLE

In the introduction to the book "Revitalizing A Nation" published by the Heritage Foundation, Inc., 1952, Norman Vincent Peale, D.D., wrote, "No man of our time is more authentically the voice of real America than Douglas MacArthur. To the millions who lined the streets of our great cities to cheer and weep as he passed by, he is the personification of American tradition and history.

"As he rode up great avenues 'midst vast throngs, the people through misty eyes saw in him the noble leaders of the past - Washington, Lee, Grant. And when he addressed the Congress of the United States, once again Americans heard the great truths which many, starved for them, never expected to hear again, and those who never heard them before wept unashamedly.

"In this stalwart, romantic figure, the great hopes, dreams and ideals of our country come to life again. He stimulates renewed faith that the land of Washington, Jefferson and Lincoln still lives in the hearts of the people."

Following Dr. Peale's introduction, John M. Pratt of The Heritage Foundation wrote: "Belatedly the American people are beginning dimly to sense that, emerging from World War II, are two dynamic and irreconcilable forces striving for mastery - the free world and international Communism.

"The foundation stones of the nation are the concepts and principles of the Judeo-Christian traditions and faith. Americans are free men. Their first allegiance is to their Creator - a Creator who endowed them with inalienable rights and an immortal end. Being free men it has been and is all but impossible for Americans to comprehend the basic tenets of international Communism, namely that people - human beings - are without individual entity or worth; that men are mere pawns, chattels, slaves of the States; that the State is without geographical location; that it has no national boundaries; that it encompasses the world."

This work on the wisdom and sayings of Douglas MacArthur is presented as a neo-classicist document in that almost every item listed came from the mouth of General MacArthur and from his writings. Nothing is included (accept as noted) which may not be found in biographies of MacArthur or history books which claim to reflect something MacArthur said. Taking the view of one of England's greatest writers of splendid prose in history, art, architecture and literature, John Ruskin states, "The only true history is that which is spoken out of the mouth of the person who was there, saw and did the things written about."

Douglas MacArthur wrote almost all his own speeches and there is eloquence in all of them. Calling special attention to those speeches with significant meaning that will stand the test of time are the following: the speech he made on the deck of the Missouri September 2, 1945, after taking the surrender of the Japanese; his speech before Congress after his unfortunate dismissal as a Five Star General following his tour of duty in Korea in 1951; and his magnificent speech to the Corp of Cadets of the U.S. Military Academy at West Point on May 12, 1962. These three stand out as note-worthy because they were made immediately after periods of great historical significance. In these speeches as in so many of his other speeches, he seemed to be speaking strictly from his heart.

Regardless of the individual's attitude toward politics, religion, military or civilian service, MacArthur's words sound spiritual, practical. His political thinking will stand the test of time. His life in service to his country is as one who has seen, and accomplished much; perhaps more than any other man in history.

These sayings, maxims and jewels of wisdom should be made available to children and adults alike. The sayings emphasize the importance of character, dedication, honesty and scholarship - the many personal characteristics wholly imbedded in the hearts of the men who forged our Declaration of Independence. In the Preamble to the Constitution and the Constitution, the founding fathers set the style, the direction and the ultimate goals that would lead to freedom and liberty for all our people. General MacArthur, in his pronouncements, sets the tone, and direction we must follow to insure these freedoms are never abrogated by unsavory political elements in our society experimenting with ways to relieve us of our liberty for political advantage through insidious, and illegal mandates to carry out their own agenda - in most cases counter to the values in our Constitution.

To assist the reader in finding elements in this book which may satisfy a particular need for guidance, the MacArthur Wisdoms and Visions have been listed in categories; i.e., The Athlete, Building Character, Corregidor, Education, the Family, Foreign Policy, Government, Life, Peace, The Philippines, Politics, Religion, The Soldier and War.

There is only one saying in this work that definitely is not original with MacArthur. The saying taken from MacArthur's favorite Philosopher Plato, "Only the dead have seen the last of war." Each time MacArthur used this expression, however, he gave Plato credit for it. MacArthur stated on many occasions he believed Plato to be the greatest philosopher of all time. He read Plato extensively.

Regarding the expression "Only the dead have seen the last of war," historians and statisticians will be hard pressed to find a decade in the history of civilization when war, somewhere on earth was not in progress. MacArthur's detailed review of war and peace in history for the past 3000 years reflect a conclusion - war was taking place somewhere in this world except for a total of 268 years. MacArthur refers to this expression in so many of his speeches about the role of the military and politics in the overall function of the Federal establishment. He rebuts the liberal thought that the military press for funds to aggrandize themselves and develop sophisticated equipment of destruction to impress the world on the ability of the military to "kill people and break things." On this level of thinking MacArthur says the military above all people despise war because it is they who must take the first blow and are the first to be scarred in time of war. MacArthur further states the best and only way to prevent war, as far as the United States is concerned, is to make and keep America the strongest military force in the world. America must realize only a powerful American military presence throughout the world can ensure our security. Only the military can ensure our country's future. It is the primary and most important element in our Constitution. The President cannot ensure our security - the Congress cannot - the economy cannot - Wall Street cannot - the colleges and universities with all their superior intelligence cannot and the people cannot unless they have a ready, well-trained, dedicated, patriotic and well-manned military in place at all times. The military academies are an essential element in America's great world wide concerns. From these academies come the great leaders of the future who will hold the country together. Without them the decline and fall of America would be inevitable. To call on John Ruskin again - as early as 1850 he wrote, "Five great intellectual professions have hitherto existed in every civilized nation: 1. The soldiers to defend it; 2. The merchants to provide for it; 3. The pastors to teach it; 4. The physicians to keep it in health; 5. The lawyers to enforce justice in it. And the duty of all of these is, on due occasion, to die for it."

We leave it to each reader of this work to decide for themselves which of these five intellectual areas may be failing us. It is significant to note Ruskin's order of listing. It is our Constitution which stresses the importance and imperative of security for our country and only the military can ensure that. It was not by chance that Ruskin listed the professions in the order shown, but the result of his keen mind, philosophical thinking and vision. Logic alone can be seen as the progressive need for each in order of its significance in securing the nation. Would "you" be willing to die for your country?

Throughout this work you will find threads which lead back to time immemorial; to the great philosophers and teachers of early Greek history - the Romans and eventually to our great first President and father of our country, George Washington.

MacArthur was well read. He has stated in his own autobiography as principally one who read non-fiction. Only rarely did he read fiction. In his earlier days he devoted part of his reading time to the classics; Shakespeare, Thomas Mann. The great philosophers and writers of classical history of Greece and Rome were well known to him and many of his sayings and maxims emanated from earlier times.

General Douglas MacArthur accomplished many things in his lifetime. More, some say, than any other man in the history of civilization. The record is there for all to see. More books have been written about MacArthur (during his lifetime) than for any other man in history. MacArthur is quoted or referred to in literally thousands of clippings, magazine articles, history books, books on politics, books on economics; more than any other man in the history of civilization. Most in his lifetime. He was, as stated by Norman Vincent Peale, "The very heart and soul of America." MacArthur was endowed with broad vision and acquired great knowledge of the past. He used this knowledge to make remarkable predictions of future events.

It is important to note that MacArthur did not only write these wonderful maxims and mouth the noteworthy and provocative sayings, but he actually lived them religiously throughout his life. The two individuals who knew MacArthur best over a long period of time and under the most trying periods in our history and his - World War I and World War II, lived with him, served close to him through a myriad of dangerous, emotional and physically straining situations are the best to judge his performance under these conditions, have confirmed these facts. The two individuals referred to are Jean MacArthur, his wife, and General George C. Kenney, his Air Force Commander in WWII. Most historians and biographers of MacArthur have written after the conclusion of their work - "no one really knows MacArthur." He is an enigma to most people who do not like him. They try to find ways to criticize him and without basis. MacArthur was in fact a master of disguise.

His private life was, on the other hand, relaxed, gentle, caring, selfless, thoughtful of others and showed grave concern for all the men he must send into battle. He was pleasant to be with and enjoyed banter with those closest to him. He was surprisingly shy around strangers especially at cocktail parties, dances and other (necessary) social activities. He was a loving, faithful husband and father.

He was in public the man the people wanted to see - a stalwart character of iron and steel stature - firm convictions - charisma so powerful and endearing to the public they would openly cry streams of tears on his passing in parade or standing still as a bronze statue in their presence. My research and personal knowledge of the man uncovered a number of individuals who had the courage to express their strong feelings on MacArthur. Surprisingly the statements were made over different periods in our recent history, and there is no indication they are in any way connected, the statement is: "MacArthur is the greatest man in history." The principal individuals who have made such a statement, and all can be found published in history books, biographies, news articles and magazine articles. A short list follows:

"The greatest man who ever lived except Jesus Christ" and "The greatest General in world history" General George Stratemeyer, his Air Force Chief in Japan and Korea, 1951;

"The man I would follow anywhere blindfolded" Gen. Jonathan Wainwright, U.S. Army, his former corp commander in the Philippines, at the Japanese surrender ceremonies, September 2, 1945;

"The most selfless man I have ever known" Gen. George C. Kenney, U.S.A.F., Commander, Allied Forces Southwest Pacific in World War II, 1950;

"The greatest American ever" Brig. Gen. Carlos Romulus, U.S. Army;

"The greatest" Col. Edward T. Imparato, U.S.A.F.;

"MacArthur has a solid claim to greatness" Stephen E. Ambrose, Historian, author of military books;

"The greatest man alive" Major Gen. Edward Almond, U.S. Army;

"MacArthur is the greatest leader of troops we have and I intend to make him a Division Commander" General John Pershing, U.S. Army, during WW I.

MacArthur built his own image. Individuals who had the good fortune to spend time in his presence came away with staunch praise for his many positive positions about the state of the nation - the state of politics in America - the need for a strong defense and his great love of the Army, its great enlisted corp and forever the long gray line. He would not only talk about these great and important facets of our lives, but where weakness was apparent he could and would offer positive solutions. His method of interaction with his visitor was to pace the floor while describing his view of the present situation and also the future. In every reference in history books, biographies, and magazine articles a visit with MacArthur was an event.

His command of the English language was unsurpassed. His cadence, his inflections, his phrasing, his tone, would surpass the performance of the best actors of stage and screen. War correspondent William Allen White, on an unusual occasion immediately after the end of WW I, chanced to be passing MacArthur's headquarters during his occupation duty in Germany with his renowned 42nd Infantry Division in Germany. White stopped by to take advantage of his presence there to pay his respects to MacArthur. He had never met MacArthur but had heard so many stories about him. He thought the surprise visit would truly test the metal of the officer by catching him off guard. On entering the headquarters (living quarters) he asked if MacArthur was available. The aide said he was lying down feeling ill but he would check. White surveyed the quarters and found the decor very austere, very plain and all white. The owner of the house was a German Baron who maintained a friendly but formal attitude with the staff of officers billeted there. White reflects on this visit as follows: "Into this austere and formal setting flashed General MacArthur, aged thirty-eight a bachelor, with the grace and charm of a stage hero. I had never before met so vivid, so captivating, so magnetic a man. He was all that Barrymore and John Drew hoped to be. And how he could talk. He was a West Pointer, son of the old general, General Fred Funston's friend and was widely read. He stood six feet and had a clean shaven face, a clean cut mouth, nose and chin, lots of brown hair, good eyes with a 'come hither' in them, that must have played the devil with the girls, and yet he was as 'he' as chapman's bull in the Estes Park meadows. His staff adored him his men worshiped him, and he seemed to be entirely without vanity. He was lounging in his room, not well (an ulcer in his throat) and he wore a ragged brown sweater and civilian pants - nothing more. He was greatly against the order prohibiting fraternization. He said the order only hurt the boys."

This report by William Allen White, a noted war correspondent and respected journalist, should set the record straight on whether or not MacArthur was a pompous, egotistical, arrogant and selfish man.

It was only 23 years later that the writer met MacArthur at Melbourne, Australia, on his arrival there after MacArthur was ordered to leave the Philippines. From that date forward to the end of World War II on MacArthur's arrival at Atsugi, Japan on August 30, 1945, to accept the Japanese surrender, we had the opportunity to observe him in various modes, places and operations and never did I see him in a characterization other than that eloquence described by William Allen White and MacArthur was 62 years old in 1942.

His character, his demeanor, his posture, his honesty, his compassion were frozen in place after being well-honed during his four years as a Cadet at West Point. West Point's primary mission is the development of character. MacArthur is the model for all America.

An analysis of all of his listed sayings - most of which came from his speeches after his return to the United States - can be traced back to his early days in high school, his West Point years and his experiences during World War I. Psychologists and psychiatrists have recorded that man's character traits become fully developed by age 20. If this is so most of the negative comments about MacArthur can be discounted. The pomposity, the egotist, the arrogance, the lying and many more can be attributed primarily to idle gossip, misinterpretation of his motive, the result of disparaging remarks by individuals who have been somehow offended by some personal or official action by MacArthur essential for maximum effectiveness related to military operations and duties.

Many of the negatives about MacArthur can be traced to three situations; the misunderstanding by the media and public concerning his duties and responsibilities in quelling the riots and instability in the bonus march on Washington, the basic conflict with Truman and the early days of World War II. The military situation in the Far East was precarious, desperate in fact. The maximum effort on all personnel was essential and failure due to ineffective performance, lack of attention to duty, slack leadership, lack of will and determination usually resulted in many officers - some of very high rank - junior and senior staffs and enlisted ranks were summarily dismissed and replaced by more competent individuals. The many who felt pressed failed to heed the motto - Duty, Honor Country - and could not be depended on in the heat of battle. It was at this stage that such expressions as "Dugout Doug" surfaced - not realizing, of course, that MacArthur was the man who received the most decorations for gallantry in action, than any other person in American history. That he stood under the flag on Corregidor every night when the Japanese bombers carried on their almost nightly air raids to soften the little island for their planned amphibious landing. Nor were they aware of MacArthur's great leadership in world War I; leading his regiments into battle at the front of his troops refusing to wear a steel helmet and armed only with a walking stick. MacArthur was honored by France, England and the United States as one of the most daring and effective commanders and bravest soldiers in World War I. Even his staff honored MacArthur on his departure from his beloved 42nd Infantry Division with a gold cigarette case inscribed and etched with the words, "The Bravest Of The Brave". The French and American leaders at the end of World War I assigned MacArthur the honor in print as the best Damn General in World War I.

The record reflects the facts from personal experience, from war correspondence, from visiting dignitaries, from U. S. Army, Air Force, Navy officers of high rank that any one visiting MacArthur for at least one hour of conversation came away with the same general impression received from William Allen White's report. These documented facts would naturally lead one to believe the negative comments about MacArthur must emanate from innuendos, hearsay, misunderstood official acts by MacArthur and not by someone who actually saw the arrogance, the egotism, the pomposity. As negative stories and gossip moves along from mouth to ear - from ear to mouth, it grows and grows and gets more vicious with each telling.

In the final analysis it was General George C. Kenney who set the record straight in 1952 by writing his book "The MacArthur I Know". General Kenney was confounded by the many insulting and negative stories reflecting the feelings of many who did not like MacArthur. Any great leader will have detractors for a variety of reasons - most of them personal, and most of them dead wrong. Kenney took the necessary time after World War II to trace the source and the reasons for most of the negativism about MacArthur. His findings convinced him that all the cases he had time to pursue were based on fabrication by MacArthur's enemies, misinterpretation of MacArthur's motives and intentions, hearsay, contrived situations by individuals intent on official harm to MacArthur's reputation for their own political gain (Truman). General Kenney's book is well researched and his conclusions should put to rest forever the malicious condemnation of America's greatest hero. Continuing research on MacArthur uncovered the basic source for General Kenney's very positive final report on MacArthur.

MacArthur's devotion to his troops both officers and men, is legendary. In all his speeches that relate to military operation - be it training, occupation, duty or actual combat - his feeling for his men never wavered. In a speech to his beloved

42nd Rainbow Infantry Division, July 14, 1935, MacArthur stated, "It was with you I lived my greatest moments. It is of you I have my greatest memories." This is a true and honest reflection of his lifelong enduring and deep felt love of his officers and men. These words were not made for the purpose of pandering to his men or to impress the public with the warmth of his feelings. It was the result of his close living with his troops. MacArthur lived among them in bivouac and was side by side with them in battle. He was among the few high ranking officers who led his troops into battle from the front, not from headquarters in the rear. He honestly and sincerely loved the troops. It certainly was not a slip of the tongue or by a casual remark that the WW I Secretary of War stated in public MacArthur was the greatest fighting General in World War I.

This great devotion for his men carried through from World War I to World War II when again he had the opportunity to work with troops in battle.

At the onset of military action on Luzon in the Philippines early in the WW II, MacArthur forces consisted of four untrained Army divisions; two American and two Philippine. The Japanese landed 100,000 troops at Lingayen Gulf. Hopelessly out manned and out gunned and no possibility of reinforcements reaching the Philippines in time to halt the onslaught, MacArthur could only initiate a massive retrograde action to slow the progress of Japanese forces toward Manila and Corregidor. Roosevelt had promised reinforcements would soon arrive to support his operation but none arrived. The two Divisions slated for his command were diverted to Australia because Washington considered sending troops to MacArthur at this stage pure folly.

Japanese commanders expected a quick victory in the Philippines. The Japanese Army was commanded by one of their most able generals. However, MacArthur's magnificently executed retrograde action stalled the Japanese advance to Manila in one of the most significant holding actions ever executed by any Army under similar circumstances anywhere in the past. Japanese records reflect their planned advance to capture Manila was to last five weeks. In reality it took General Masaharu Homma five months to subdue the defending forces with his greatly superior forces.

MacArthur's many thoughtful and provocative sayings were not pure rhetoric. They were statements in his speeches for people to contemplate and to live by - and they were not for his audience alone. They were axioms and rules by which he lived his own life. His sayings can be traced back to some teaching in MacArthur's own life and experience. They were his rules for the way he wanted to live his own life.

The accolades MacArthur received over a period of years from his time at West Point as a student to and through his World War I and World War II experiences as a fighting General were so numerous it would take a full size book to cover them all. The compliments, awards and private praise came from many sources over the long career of this soldier statesman. A brief and almost passing comment or two will illustrate the reaction from a short association with him. This brief "aside" from David Halberstain's book "The Powers That Be", published by Alfred A. Knopf, Inc., in 1979, is as follows: "Time's heroes during the late forties and early fifties were men like Foster Dulles and Douglas MacArthur, who talked of bringing moral standards to foreign affairs. Of MacArthur, time was particularly worshipful. In that period when he was the

Consul General of Japan inside the Dai Ichi building, once the heart of a Japanese insurance empire, bleary-eyed staff officers looked up from stacks of papers, whispered proudly, "God, the man is great." Major General Almond, his Chief of Staff, said straight out, "he's the greatest man alive." Reverent Air Force General George E. Stratemeyer put it as strongly as it could be put, "...he's the greatest man in history." This type of praise openly spoken and written into history by many individuals who had the good fortune to work closely with MacArthur, gives great credit to the man and his many accomplishments. The authors of the praise are at a loss to understand the false, misleading and vicious verbal attacks against a man considered by most Americans as the greatest American in history.

Rhee-MacArthur Memorial Park in Seoul, Korea.

THE ATHLETE

From personal knowledge and intimate experience, I know how immeasurably Football has contributed over the years to American leadership on the battlefield. Just as in war, the very essence of success on the gridiron is a combination of physical prowess and skill, close coordination of men and maneuver and that indomitable courage which alone can produce the will to victory. I can repeat with the added conviction of time what I said many long years ago on the Plain at West Point: "On the fields of friendly strife are sown the seeds that on other fields and other days will bring forth victory."

Touchdown Club Annual Dinner,
New York City, New York,
December 6, 1951

If I were to give you but one word of warning, it would be to keep Football, and for that matter all other American sports, free of governmental bureaucratic regulation.

Touchdown Club Annual Dinner,
New York City, New York,
December 6, 1951

I am of the football vintage of Walter Camp and Alonzo Stagg. I have thrilled to the blaze of Hinckey and Hefflefinger, of Haughton and Brickley, of Poe and Trenchard and Hare. I collaborated with Charlie Daly and Pot Graves and Bull Halsey, later to become our peerless fighting Admiral and my beloved comrade-in-arms of the Pacific, was then a Midshipman back. I raised McEwan and Oliphant, Neyland and Blaik. I learned the hard way from Knute Rockne and Gipp and the Four Horsemen - and every year on every campus and every field throughout the land, I can see their counterparts. I can see their great ideals and performances being repeated over and over again - year on year - and, as each passes on, I find myself again and again with the same old catch in my throat, the same old pounding in my heart, the same old yell on my lips, "Well done, Mr. Football. Yours is the Touchdown."

Touchdown Club Annual Dinner,
New York City, New York,
December 6, 1951

Editor's note: General MacArthur had these words carved on the stone portals of the gymnasium at the U. S. Military Academy, West Point, New York
Upon the fields of friendly strife
Are sown the seeds
That, upon other fields, on other days
Will bear the fruits of victory.

The game (football) has become a symbol of our country's best qualities - courage, stamina, coordinated efficiency.

Annual Football Hall of Fame Dinner,
New York, New York,
December 1, 1959

MacArthur with "Red Bliak" at the Army versus Syracuse game, September 1957.

CHARACTER

Duty, honor, country - Those three hallowed words reverently dictate what you ought to be, what you can be, what you will be. They are your rallying point to build courage when courage seems to fail, to regain faith when there seems to be little cause for faith, to create hope when hope becomes forlorn.

U. S. Military Academy,
West Point, New York,
May 12, 1962

...to be serious yet never to take yourself too seriously.

U. S. Military Academy,
West Point, New York,
May 12, 1962

Be modest so that you will remember the simplicity of true greatness, the open mind of true wisdom, the meekness of true strength.

U. S. Military Academy,
West Point, New York,
May 12, 1962

Have...a goal that is high.

U. S. Military Academy,
West Point, New York,
May 12, 1962

During my long national service, I have... had to listen and listen, and listen.

General of the Army Douglas MacArthur
"Reminiscences"
McGraw-Hill Book Company, New York, 1964

They (duty, honor, country) give you a temperamental predominance of courage over timidity.

U. S. Military Academy,
West Point, New York,
May 12, 1962

...to learn to stand up in the storm, but have compassion on those who fail.

U. S. Military Academy,
West Point, New York,
May 12, 1962

Learn to laugh yet never forget how to weep.

U. S. Military Academy,
West Point, New York,
May 12, 1962

Never talk more than is necessary.
General of the Army Douglas MacArthur
"Reminiscences"
McGraw-Hill Book Company, New York, 1964

My father and mother had taught me those two immutable principles - never to lie, never to tattle.
General of the Army Douglas MacArthur
"Reminiscences"
McGraw-Hill Book Company, New York, 1964

Nobody grows old by merely living a number of years. People grow old only by deserting their ideals. Years may wrinkle the skin, but to give up interest wrinkles the soul. .... In the central place of every heart there is a recording chamber; so long as it receives messages of beauty, hope and cheer and courage, so long are you young. When the wires are all down and your heart is covered with the snows of pessimism and the ice of cynicism, then and then only, are you old.
Los Angeles County Council,
American Legion, Los Angeles, California,
January 26, 1955

It (renunciation of war) must be effected by action - not words alone...
Allied Council for Japan,
April 5, 1946

The highest standards of honor were to be demanded as the only solid foundation for a military career.
General of the Army Douglas MacArthur
"Reminiscences"
McGraw-Hill Book Company, New York, 1964

... a code of individual conduct which would maintain ... a personal responsibility to his mates, to his community, and above all to his country.
General of the Army Douglas MacArthur
"Reminiscences"
McGraw-Hill Book Company, New York, 1964

In the final analysis of the West Point product, character is the most precious component.
General of the Army Douglas MacArthur
"Reminiscences"
McGraw-Hill Book Company, New York, 1964

...be proud and unbending in honest failure, but humble and gentle in success.
U. S. Military Academy,
West Point, New York,
May 12, 1962

...not to substitute words for actions ...
U. S. Military Academy,
West Point, New York,
May 12, 1962

Be modest so that you will remember the simplicity of true greatness, the open mind of true wisdom, the meekness of true strength.
U. S. Military Academy,
West Point, New York,
May 12, 1962

I shall set my course to the end that no man need fear to speak the truth.
Massachusetts Legislature,
Boston, Massachusetts,
July 25, 1951

... that truth replace false and slanted propaganda in public information.
Fort Worth, Texas,
June 16, 1951

... that fear and timidity be repudiated as having no place in shaping our destiny.
Fort Worth, Texas,
June 16, 1951

The drift away from the truth is leaving the people confused and bewildered.
Fort Worth, Texas,
June 16, 1951

If we meet the challenge we cannot fail.
Massachusetts Legislature,
Boston, Massachusetts,
July 25, 1951

(We must) ... preserve inviolate those great principles and ideals of moral authority upon which is based the American way of life.
National Convention, The American Legion,
Miami, Florida,
October 17, 1951

Are we going to permit a continuing decline in public and private morality or reestablish high ethical standards as the means of regaining a diminishing faith in the integrity of our public and private institutions?
Cleveland, Ohio,
September 6, 1951

If the historian of the future should deem my service worthy of some slight reference, it would be my hope that he mention me not as a Commander engaged in campaigns and battles, even though victorious to American arms, but rather as that one whose sacred duty it became, once the guns were silenced, to carry to the land of our vanquished foe the solace and hope and faith of Christian morals. Could I have but a line a century hence crediting a contribution to the advance of peace, I would gladly yield every honor which has been accorded by war.

National Institute of Social Sciences upon
being awarded the Society's Gold Medal,
Waldorf- Astoria Hotel, New York, NY
November 8, 1951,

This carnival (Socialism) of special privilege cannot fail to undermine our heritage of character.

Opening, Centennial Celebration,
Seattle, Washington,
November 13, 1951

(On our soldiers' performance in Korea) Theirs is a cause and a limitation which requires both courage and determination, and I can report to you they have met the test in every way.

City Hall,
San Francisco, California,
April 18, 1951

When I joined the Army even before the turn of the century, it was the fulfillment of all my boyish hopes and dreams.

Address to Congress,
Washington, DC,
April 19, 1951

I have been encouraged in many ways by the events which have followed my return from long absence abroad. Foremost of the encouraging signs has been the demonstration that the American people are keenly alive to their own responsibilities and unhesitatingly voice their views on the direction of the policy of government. It is for future events to ascertain whether they still retain the ultimate authority over government as intended by the Constitution or whether such authority has been lost in the drift from the pattern ordained by the architects of our political institutions.

Chicago, Illinois,
April 26, 1951

My correspondence reflects a growing lack of faith by a large segment of our population in the responsibility and moral fiber of our own process of government. Truth has ceased to be keystone to the arch of our national conscience and propaganda has replaced it as the rallying media for public support.

Texas Legislature,
Austin, Texas,
June 13, 1951

Corruption and rumors of corruption have shaken the people's trust in the integrity of those administering the civil power.

Texas Legislature,
Austin, Texas,
June 13, 1951

Before the descendants of these early American patriots I am honored, indeed, to address this legislative assembly in response to its thoughtful and kind invitation. I do so with neither partisan affiliation nor political purpose.

But I have been warned by many that an outspoken course, even if it be solely of truth, will bring down upon my head ruthless retaliation - that efforts will be made to destroy public faith in the integrity of my views - not by force of just argument but by the application of the false methods of propaganda. I am told in effect I must follow blindly the leader - keep silent - or take the bitter consequences.

I had thought Abraham Lincoln had pinned down for all time this ugly code when he declared: "To sin by silence when they should protest makes cowards of men."

I shall raise my voice as loud and as often as I believe it to be in the interest of the American people. I shall dedicate all of my energies to restoring to American life those immutable principles and ideals which your forebears and mine handed down to us in sacred trust. I shall assist in the regaining of that moral base for both public and private life which will restore the people's faith in the integrity of public institutions and the private faith of ever man in the integrity of his neighbor.

I shall set my course to the end that no man need fear to speak the truth. I could not do less, for the opportunities for service my country has given me and the honors it has conferred upon me have imposed an obligation which is not discharged by the termination of public service.

Massachusetts Legislature,
Boston, Massachusetts,
July 25, 1951

It was the adventurous spirit of Americans which despite risks and hazards carved a great nation from an almost impenetrable wilderness; which established the pattern for modern industrialization and scientific development; which built our own almost unbelievable material progress and favorably influenced that of all others; which through the scientific advance of means of communication closed the international geographic gap to permit rapid and effective trade and commerce among the peoples of the world; which raised the living standard of the American people beyond that ever before known; and which elevated the laborer, the farmer and the tradesman to their rightful station of dignity and relative prosperity.

Massachusetts Legislature,
Boston, Massachusetts,
July 25, 1951

Public morality is the touchstone to the people's faith in the integrity of the governmental process.

Letter to the Prime Minister of Japan,
August 20, 1951

Are we going to permit a continuing decline in public and private morality or reestablish high ethical standards as the means of regaining a diminishing faith in the integrity of our public and private institutions?

Cleveland, Ohio,
September 6, 1951

If the historian of the future should deem my service worthy of some slight reference, it would be my hope that he mention me not as a Commander engaged in campaigns and battles, even though
victorious to American arms, but rather as that one whose sacred duty it became, once the guns were silenced, to carry to the land of our vanquished foe the solace and hope and faith of Christian morals. Could I have but a line a century hence crediting a contribution to the advance of peace, I would gladly yield every honor which has been accorded to war.

National Institute of Social Sciences
Annual Dinner,
Waldorf-Astoria Hotel, New York City, New York
November 8, 1951

The people have it in their hands to restore morality, wisdom and vision to the direction of our foreign and domestic affairs and regain the religious base which in times past assured general integrity in public and private life.

Opening, Centennial Celebration,
Seattle, Washington,
November 13, 1951

I have faith that the American people will not be fooled - that they will demand that the national policy be charted to a course of international realism without regard to domestic political expediency.

Opening, Centennial Celebration,
Seattle, Washington,
November 13, 1951

We must condemn those who would corrupt the principles of individual liberty, freedom's mighty instrument of spiritual power. We must not view with indifference men of base of weak character, who do not fulfill their public stewardship.

Receiving "Award for Service to Humanity"
from the Salvation Army,
New York, New York,
December 12, 1951

I am profoundly grateful for the honor you do me - an honor whose deep significance rests upon its association with the anniversary of the birth of that peerless American patriot, Benjamin Franklin. Nothing which I might say could add luster to the exalted stature of this great man. For there is indelibly etched in detail upon the pages of history the record of his monumental works. His life exemplifies, possibly more than that of any other, the boundless opportunity with which Americans have been endowed since this continent became a sanctuary from tyranny and oppression.

Receiving the "Gold Medal of Achievement"
award from the Poor Richard Club of
Philadelphia at a meeting held in
New York, New York,
January 15, 1952

Morality was easily the cardinal virtue which characterized his (Benjamin Franklin) long years of public service, and he held justice to be "the surest foundation on which to erect and establish a new state."

Receiving the "Gold Medal of Achievement"
award from the Poor Richard Club of
Philadelphia at a meeting held in
New York, New York,
January 15, 1952

Let a leadership then emerge with the vision and moral courage to discard the dogma of political precedent which seeks to be all things to all people - a leadership firmly resolved to restore political morality; regain thrift and frugality as the cornerstone to national stability and progress; re-establish the diffusion of the political power; shore up the sagging beams of our free institutions; revitalize the battered remnants of our personal freedoms; reorient foreign policy to reality and reason; and renew a devotion to God and the religious base upon which our country was erected.

Mississippi Legislature,
Jackson, Mississippi,
March 22, 1952

Few men have had so poignant an opportunity to see and evaluate our great resource of industrial power. In the violence of our last three wars abroad, when our country's very destiny hung in the balance, I have seen the sinews of battle pour from your factories in massive quantities to bring victory to American colors where otherwise defeat might well have been. This has not sprung so much from great advantage in raw resource, nor indeed, from any complete monopoly in wisdom and scientific knowledge, but more than all else, it has come from the character of this mighty blend of the universe known as the American people.

Michigan Legislature,
Lansing, Michigan,
May 15, 1952

I have seen that character indelibly etched upon the faces of the millions I have met from North to South, from east to West; a spiritual character which seeks the supremacy of right over wrong; a determined character which will not yield the inalienable right of personal liberty; an aggressive character which has surmounted all obstacles in the forging upon this continent of a dynamic civilization which is at once the wonder, the inspiration and the envy of the world.

Michigan Legislature,
Lansing, Michigan,
May 15, 1952

The basic character of the American people is the energizing force behind America's past, the stabilizing influence to America's present and the main hope of America's future.

Michigan Legislature,
Lansing, Michigan,
May 15, 1952

Despite stresses and strains, the fine basic character of the American people remains unimpaired.

Keynote Address,
Republican National Convention,
Chicago, Illinois,
July 7, 1952

I have an abiding faith in the future of this nation - a faith grounded in the invincible character of the American people. It has never failed to triumph in our hours of national adversity and peril; and, as it has in the past, it will again restore to our land the serenity of hope without fear. To such end, I am happy indeed to be among so distinguished a company as this, charged in the service of our beloved country with so primary a responsibility for the course of our destiny as a free, happy and prosperous people.

National Association of Manufacturers,
Waldorf-Astoria Hotel, New York, New York,
December 5, 1952

Only those are fit to live who are not afraid to die.

Veterans of The Rainbow (42nd) Infantry
Division of World War I,
Washington, DC,
July 14, 1935

He (the American soldier) belongs to posterity as the instructor of future generations in the principles of liberty and right.

Veterans of The Rainbow (42nd) Infantry
Division of World War I,
Washington, DC,
July 14, 1935

The problem basically is theological and involves a spiritual recrudescence and improvement of human character that will synchronize with our almost matchless advance in science, art, literature and all material and cultural development.

VJ Day Broadcast, U.S.S. Missouri,
September 2, 1945

Our great strength rests in those high-minded and patriotic Americans whose faith in God and love of country transcends all selfish and self-serving instincts. We must command their maximum effort toward a restoration to public and private relationships of our age-old standards of morality and ethics - a return to the religious fervor which animated our leadership of former years to chart a course of humility and integrity as best to serve the public interest.

Receiving "Award for Service to Humanity"
from the Salvation Army,
New York, New York,
December 12, 1951

If the national well being is to be served it is for us of this generation, as indeed for Americans of every generation, to assess the current strength of the pioneering spirit and appraise anew the incentives which alone can give it dynamic vitality. In so doing, it is well that we remember the composite of pioneering characteristics which have gone into the building of the great Pacific coast. Here strength overcame weakness, courage dominated fear, and the responsibility of life overshadowed the certainty of death. Here men, through an exemplification of spirituality, fashioned character as a far more meaningful and valued heritage than the material results their labors brought forth. It is that heritage of character which must be preserved by our generation so that we could do now what they did then.

Opening, Centennial Celebration,
Seattle, Washington,
November 13, 1951

This is an era characterized by a universal sentiment of nationalism. This we must respect if we would gain the respect of others. The peoples of the world will only follow our leadership upon the basis of our moral integrity and spiritual as well as physical strength.

They will measure us not by the monies we recklessly give them, but by the general attitudes with which we face the common problems of mankind.

Mississippi Legislature,
Jackson, Mississippi,
March 22, 1952

MacArthur Memorial in Tucklham, Leyte.

Indivisible from this trend and probably contributory to it, is a growing tendency to overlook certain forms of laxity in high quarters. Petty corruption in the public administration is a disease unfortunately common to all nations but I refer to an even more alarming situation.

Men of significant stature in national affairs appear to cower before the threat of reprisal if the truth be expressed in criticism of those in higher public authority.

For example, I find in existence a new and heretofore unknown and dangerous concept that the members of our armed forces owe primary allegiance and loyalty to those who temporarily exercise the authority of the executive branch of government, rather than to the country and its constitution which they are to defend.

No proposition could be more dangerous. None could cast greater doubt upon the integrity of the armed services.

For its application would at once convert them from their traditional and constitutional role as the instrument for the defense of the Republic into something partaking of the nature of a pretorian guard owing sole allegiance to the political master of the hour.

While for the purpose of administration and command the armed services are within the executive branch of the government, they are accountable as well to the Congress, charged with the policy making responsibility, and to the people, ultimate repository of all national power.

Yet so inordinate has been the application of the executive power that members of the armed services have been subjected to the most arbitrary and ruthless treatment for daring to speak the truth in accordance with conviction and conscience.

Massachusetts Legislature,
Boston, Massachusetts,
July 25, 1951

Truth has ceased to be the keystone to the arch of our national conscience and propaganda has replaced it as the rallying media for public support. Corruption and rumors of corruption have shaken the people's trust in the integrity of those administering the civil power.

Texas Legislature,
Austin, Texas,
June 13, 1951

I have just crossed the continent in hours, where it took those who first pioneered the way as many long, tortuous and perilous months. Seattle proudly and majestically stands today at one hundred years of age full beneficiary of what the pioneering spirit has wrought upon this continent. It marks the fruition of the dream to bring the fruits of civilization to a vast and then uncharted wilderness. It has become a heritage which all Americans may share with pride and hope. The inspiration to be drawn from its one hundred years of the past builds faith in the next hundred years of the future.

Opening, Centennial Celebration,
Seattle, Washington,
November 13, 1951

Many pessimistic voices are being raised today throughout the land. But the times are full of hope if the vision and courage and faith of the early pioneer continue to animate the American people in the discharge of their sovereign responsibilities.

The people have it in their hands to restore morality, wisdom and vision to the direction of our foreign and domestic affairs and regain the religious base which in times past assured general integrity in public and private life.

Despite failures in leadership, they have it in their power to rise to that stature which befits their material strength; to reject the Socialist policies covertly and by devious means being forced upon us; to stamp out Communist influence which has played so ill-famed a part in the past misdirection of our public administration; to reorganize our government under a leadership invincibly obedient to our constitutional mandates; to reinforce existing safeguards to our economy of free enterprise; to reassert full protection for freedom of speech and expression and those other freedoms now threatened; to regain State and community autonomy; to renounce undue alien interference in the shaping of American public policy; and to re-establish our governmental process upon a foundation of faith in our American institutions, American traditions and the time-tested adequacy of American vision.

Opening, Centennial Celebration,
Seattle, Washington,
November 13, 1951

MacArthur, in a conversation with Sid Huff, one of his personal aides, at the point of departure from Corregidor showed Sid the only weapon he had; (and carried with him at all times) a Derringer double barrel pistol that could fit in your hand. MacArthur said, "Sid, they will never take me alive."

Related by Col. Sid Huff, U.S.A. in his book
"My Fifteen Years With General MacArthur,"
Paperback Library, Inc., New York.

When giving assignments to a subordinate, "You can do it; don't come back until you do."

Related by Col. Sid Huff, U.S.A. in his book
"My Fifteen Years With General MacArthur,"
Paperback Library, Inc., New York.

I hesitate to refer to my own relief from the Far Eastern Commands as I have never questioned the legal authority underlying such action. But the three sole reasons publicly stated by the highest authority clearly demonstrate the arbitrary nature of the decision.

The first reason given was that, contrary to existing policy, I warned of the strategic relationship of Formosa to American security and the dangers inherent in this area's falling under Communist control. Yet this viewpoint has since been declared by the Secretary of State, under oath before Congressional Committees, to have been and to be the invincible and long standing policy of the United States.

The second reason given was that I communicated my readiness to meet the enemy commander at any time to discuss acceptable terms of a cease fire arrangement. Yet, for this proposal, I was relieved of my command by the same authorities who since have received so enthusiastically the identical proposal when made by the Soviet Government.

The third and final reason advanced was my replying to a Congressman's request for information on a public subject then under open consideration by the Congress. Yet both Houses of Congress promptly passed a law confirming my action, which indeed had been entirely in accordance with a long existing and well recognized though unwritten policy.

This law states that no member of the Armed Forces shall be restricted or prevented from communicating directly or indirectly with any member or members of Congress concerning any subject unless such communication is in violation of law or the security and safety of the United States. And this formal enactment of basic public policy was approved without the slightest dissent by the President.

Is there wonder that men who seek an objective understanding of American policy thinking become completely frustrated and bewildered? Is there wonder that Soviet propaganda so completely dominated American foreign policy? And, indeed, what is our foreign policy?

We hear impassioned appeals that it be bi-partisan - violent charges that sinister efforts are being made to obstruct and defeat it - but I defy you or any other man to tell me what it is. It has become a mass of confused misunderstandings and vacillations. It has meant one thing today - another tomorrow. It has almost blown with every wind, changed with every tide.

The sorry truth is we have no policy. Expediencies as variable and shifting as the exigencies of the moment seem to be the only guide. Yesterday, we disarmed, today we arm and what of tomorrow? We have been told of the war in Korea that it is the wrong war, with the wrong enemy, at the wrong time and in the wrong place. Does this mean that they intend and indeed plan what they would call a right war, with a right enemy, at a right time and in a right place?

If successful in mounting the North Atlantic Pact in 1953 or 1954 or at one of the ever-changing dates fixed for its consummation, what comes then? Do we mean to throw down a gage of battle? Do we mean to continue the fantastic fiscal burden indefinitely to our inevitable exhaustion?

Is our only plan to spend and spend and spend? Do we intend to resist by force Red aggression in South East Asia if it develops? Do we intend to take over commitments in the explosive Middle East? Do we intend to enter into a series of military alliances abroad? Do we intend to actually implement by force of arms the so-called Truman Plan? These are questions that disturb us because there is no answer forthcoming. We do want and need unity and bi-partisanship in our foreign policy - but when there is no policy we can but dangerously drift.

Massachusetts Legislature,
Boston, Massachusetts,
July 25, 1951

Editor's note: MacArthur's personal assessment of his need for and passion for information and guidance on his future course in life.

In September 1893, my father was ordered to Texas. I hailed this move with delight. Housing the largest garrison I had ever seen, Fort Sam Houston guarded our southern borders and was one of the most important posts in the Army. It was here that a transformation began to take place in my development. I was enrolled in the West Texas Military Academy headed by the Reverend Allen Burlesoa, rector of the Army chapel. There came a desire to know, a seeking for the reason why, a search for the truth. Abstruse mathematics began to appear as a challenge to analysis, dull Latin and Greek seemed a gateway to the moving words of the leaders of the past, laborious historical data led to the nerve-tingling battlefields of the great captains, Biblical lessons began to open the spiritual portals of a growing faith, literature to lay bare the souls of men. My studies enveloped me, my marks went higher, and many of the school medals came my way. But I also learned how little such honors mean after one wins them.

I had always loved athletics and the spirit of competition moved me to participate in as many sports as possible. I became the quarterback on the eleven, the shortstop on the nine, the tennis champion of the campus.

General of the Army Douglas MacArthur
"Reminiscences"
McGraw-Hill Book Company, New York, 1964v

I had studied the lives of Alexander and Caesar and Napoleon, and great as these captains were, all had erred when they became the leaders of occupation forces. ...but I was assailed by the gravest misgivings. With such hazards as I anticipated, could I succeed? My doubts were to be my best safeguard, my fears my greatest strength.

General of the Army Douglas MacArthur
"Reminiscences"
McGraw-Hill Book Company, New York, 1964

The philosophy I had expressed, based upon truth that men may be destroyed by what they have and what they know, but that they may be saved by what they are, produced a most favorable result, immediate and unqualified.

General of the Army Douglas MacArthur
"Reminiscences"
McGraw-Hill Book Company, New York, 1964

Whatever faults may be inherent in the military character, evasive misrepresentation has never been one of them.

General of the Army Douglas MacArthur
"Reminiscences"
McGraw-Hill Book Company, New York, 1964

...timidity breeds conflict, and courage often prevents it.

General of the Army Douglas MacArthur
"Reminiscences"
McGraw-Hill Book Company, New York, 1964

...the one thing in this world that cannot be stopped is a sound idea.

General of the Army Douglas MacArthur
"Reminiscences"
McGraw-Hill Book Company, New York, 1964

MacArthur Memorial in Intranuros, Manila.

CORREGIDOR

Are we going to permit a continuing decline in public and private morality or reestablish high ethical standards as the means of regaining a diminishing faith in the integrity of our public and private institutions?

Cleveland, Ohio,
September 6, 1951

... hoist the colors to its peak, let no enemy ever haul them down.

Flag raising Ceremonies,
Corregidor,
March 2, 1945

Corregidor needs no comment from me. It has sounded its own story at the mouth of its guns. It has scrolled its own epitaph on enemy tablets. But through the bloody haze of its last reverberating shot I shall always see the vision of its grim, gaunt, and ghastly men, still unafraid.

Statement issued on the fall of Corregidor,
May, 1942

Bataan, with Corregidor the citadel of its integral defense, made possible all that has happened since. History, I am sure, will record it as one of the decisive battles of the world. Its long-protracted struggle enabled the Allied to gather strength. Had it not held out, Australia would have fallen, with incalculably disastrous results. Our triumphs today belong equally to that dead army. Its heroism and sacrifices have been fully acclaimed, but the great strategic results of that mighty defense are only now becoming fully apparent. It was destroyed due to its dreadful handicaps, but no army in history more fully accomplished its mission. Let no man henceforth speak of it other than as a magnificent victory.

Flag raising Ceremonies,
Corregidor,
March 2, 1945

(On the Defenders of Corregidor and Bataan) Their name and their fame has become the birthright of every child born in freedom because they died unquestioning and uncomplaining, with faith in their hearts and on their lips the hope that we would go on to victory.

In the crisis the free world faces today the lessons of Bataan and Corregidor should not be forgotten. They are written in blood for all wise men to ponder. We neglect them at our Sorrow.

From "Representative Speeches of General of
the Army Douglas MacArthur" Compiled by the
Legislative Reference Service,
Library of Congress,
April 29, 1964

EDUCATION

Reach into the future yet never neglect the past.

Speech to the West Point Cadets,
May 12, 1962

During my long national service, I have ... had to listen and listen, and listen.

General of the Army Douglas MacArthur
"Reminiscences"
McGraw-Hill Book Company, New York, 1964

It (youth) is a temper of the will, a quality of the imagination, a vigor of the emotions, it is a freshness of the deep springs of life.

Dedication of MacArthur Park,
Little Rock, Arkansas,
March 23, 1952

Mr. President, I wish to express to you my thanks and deepest appreciation for the signal honor you have bestowed upon me. The field of Social Sciences which your distinguished Society represents embraces a symposium of art, culture, humanism and divinity which leads and guides both in peace and war. Its great traditions form the bulwark of modern civilization - the fruition of all man's hopes and dreams. I think you can therefore understand my pride in having my name scrolled on your tablets. You have etched for me a memory tonight I shall never forget.

National Institute of Social Sciences upon
being awarded the Society's Gold Medal,
Waldorf-Astoria Hotel,
New York, New York,
November 8, 1951

Should the pioneering spirit cease to dominate the American character, our national progress would end.

Opening, Centennial Celebration,
Seattle, Washington,
November 13, 1951.

I have never forgotten his (Grandfather's) words, "My dear boy, nothing is sure in this life. Everything is relative."

General of the Army Douglas MacArthur
"Reminiscences"
McGraw-Hill Book Company, New York, 1964

...the tyranny nas not as yet been devised which can long resist a sound idea.

Keynote Address,
Republican National Convention,
Chicago, Illinois,
July 7, 1952

Let us regain our faith in ourselves.

Texas Legislature,
Austin, Texas,
June 13, 1951

Our country will then reassume that spiritual and moral leadership recently lost in a quagmire of political ineptitude and economic incompetence.

Opening, Centennial Celebration,
Seattle, Washington,
November 13, 1951

Of all men I have ever known my father was the one I held in deepest respect and esteem.

Chicopee Falls, Massachusetts,
July 26, 1951

The courts must function as the champion of human justice and the police power be exercised with primary regard to individual rights.

Letter to the Prime Minister of Japan,
August 20, 1951

Human freedom always find ostentatious vocal support from those most bent upon its suppression. It is essential, therefore, that there be assessed with cold and calculated realism the motivation of those who say much but do little.

Salvation Army,
New York City, New York,
December 12, 1951

MacArthur meeting with Eisenhower at the White House, March 1954.

They (the working men and women of America) must insure that Government be required to gear public policy toward a continuity of social progress, avoiding however the disease of paternalism which encourages those seeking to live by the sweat and toil, initiative and enterprise of others.

They must insure that Government be restored as the political instrumentality of all of the people by holding itself above political expediency, special privilege and the patronage of money - evils which rapidly corrupt the body politic.

They must insure that Government recapture the public faith in its stewardship of public affairs by regaining the concept that public service is a public trust. There must be a restoration of implacable honesty to the public administration and a return to that strong religious base upon which the Republic was founded.

They must insure that Government purge from the public service all Communists, their sympathizers and others who do not firmly believe in the ideal of American freedom and are unable or unwilling to work diligently for its preservation and advancement.

They must insure that Government act vigorously to shore up our defense strength, recklessly dissipated in the aftermath of the Second World War, but avoid wasteful expenditure or expenditure aimed at the primary purpose of maintaining for political reason an artificial appearance of prosperity.

They must insure that Government reorient our foreign policy to a pattern of consistency and reason based upon global, rather than limited to sectional considerations, and having primary regard to our own overriding security and public welfare.

They must insure that public policy adhere to constitutional direction as the only means by which we may achieve our own free destiny as a government of law rather than men.

They must insure that Government, backed by the military strength adequate to secure our own political and territorial integrity, offer the world a leadership of constructive ideas designed to advance the goal of universal progress and enduring peace; to protect our law abiding citizens abroad while yielding no further to international extortion or blackmail; to restore the will to victory as the cornerstone to our military policy once American arms have been committed to battle; and, while doing all reasonably within our power and means to encourage international good will and cooperation, to avoid the sending of American public resources abroad merely as a means of advancing the purposes of groups having overseas investments or other special interests.

> *City Hall,*
> *Detroit, Michigan,*
> *May 16, 1952*

Only where the concept of human liberty was most deeply rooted and greatly advanced were such minority pressures decisively thrown back.

> *National Association of Manufacturers,*
> *Waldorf-Astoria Hotel, New York, New York,*
> *December 5, 1952*

Our rate of progress in the future will be determined in identical fashion. With freedom assured, there can be no limit to the progress we can make. The new world that lies before us has no boundaries. It has no lost horizons. Its limits are as broad as the spirit and the imagination of man.

National Association of Manufacturers,
Waldorf-Astoria Hotel, New York, New York,
December 5, 1952

Education is the very bulwark of national freedom, human liberty, and political equality. It teaches us the difference between that which is right and that which is wrong.

"Representative Speeches of General of the
Army Douglas MacArthur" compiled by the
Legislative Reference Service,
Library of Congress, ordered to be printed
April 29, 1964.

It has always seemed to me that the educational work under American military occupation of the Philippines is one of the most romantic chapters in Philippine history. While some countries conquer by means of the Cross, and others subjugated by means of the sword, it remained for the United States to colonize through the agency of education.

General of the Army Douglas MacArthur
"Reminiscences"
McGraw-Hill Book Company, New York, 1964

My Father and Mother had taught me those two immutable principles - never to lie, never to tattle.

General of the Army Douglas MacArthur
"Reminiscences"
McGraw-Hill Book Company, New York, 1964

MacArthur speaks to a crowd gathered in Detroit, MI, May 1952.

FAMILY

Have a heart that is clean.

U. S. Military Academy,
West Point, New York,
May 12, 1962

Let us have the courage and faith of the Alamo.

San Antonio, Texas,
June 15, 1951

Of all men I have ever known my father was the one I held in deepest respect and esteem.

Chicopee Falls, Massachusetts,
July 26, 1951

(Referring to Korea) What a complete callousness to human feeling and soldier dignity!

Cleveland, Ohio,
September 6, 1951

I am glad, indeed, to visit once again this great capital city. It brings back poignant memories of former military service here when life was gentler and happier. Washington is a magic name. In Asia it looms over the horizon as the focal point for all eyes - the beacon for those who are seeking the way and truth and the light. In Asia too I have seen your sons serving the cause of human freedom. Indomitable in battle and restrained in occupation, their conduct throughout has reflected the high moral standards of the American home. Your pride in them can be limitless.

Washington Civic Ceremony,
April 19, 1951

It was my sainted Mother who first taught me of the gentle culture of the South and of its long and noble traditions and who infused in me a deep and lasting veneration for them which is indelibly etched upon my heart. She taught me, too a devotion to God and a love of country which have ever sustained me in my many lonely and bitter moments of decision in distant and hostile lands.

Dedication of Memorial to his Mother,
Mary Pinkney Hardy,
Norfolk, Virginia,
November 18, 1951

By far our Nation's greatest resource is our youth.

Keynote Address,
Republic National Convention,
Chicago, Illinois,
July 7, 1952

This is the greatest tragedy of all - that a national administration could have so yielded to the disease of power as to betray the youth of America.

Keynote Address,
Republic National Convention,
Chicago, Illinois,
July 7, 1952

We must not fear the return of this land of normalcy merely because of the possible temporary dislocation of our economy now so largely resting upon the production in massive quantities of the sinews of war. We must not fear to end the reckless and exhausting extravagance of government merely because it may force upon us an increase of frugality. Better if need be we increase our own thrift than leave our children and children's children a heritage of want and despair.

National Association of Manufacturers,
Waldorf-Astoria Hotel, New York, New York,
December 5, 1952

... I am prouder, infinitely prouder, to be a father. ... It is my hope that my son when I am gone will remember me not from the battle but in the home, repeating with him our simple daily prayer: "Our Father who art in heaven...."

Statement made on selection by the National
Father's Day Committee as
"Father of The Year",
June 18, 1942

Any husband will tell you that the wife absolutely rules the family.

From "Representative Speeches of General of
the Army Douglas MacArthur" Compiled by the
Legislative Reference Service,
Library of Congress,
April 29, 1964

MacArthur with General Southerland, Major General Swing and Major Langhortel.

FOREIGN POLICY

If the historian of the future should deem my service worthy of some slight reference, it would be my hope that he mention me not as a Commander engaged in campaigns and battles, even though victorious to American arms, but rather as that one whose sacred duty it became, once the guns were silenced, to carry to the land of our vanquished foe the solace and hope and faith of Christian morals. Could I have but a line a century hence crediting a contribution to the advance of peace, I would gladly yield every honor which has been accorded by war.

National Institute of Social Sciences
Annual Dinner,
Waldorf-Astoria Hotel, New York, New York,
November 8, 1951

It is my own personal opinion that the greatest political mistake we made in a hundred years in the Pacific, was in allowing the communists to grow in power in China.

I think, at one stroke, we undid everything, starting from John Hay, through Taft, Leonard Wood, Woodrow Wilson, Henry Stimson, and all those great architects of our Pacific policy.

I believe it was fundamental and I believe we will pay for it, for a century.

Testimony before the Senate Committees,
May 3, 1951
Armel Dyer
"The Oratory of Douglas MacArthur"
University of Oregon, Ph.D., 1968

... the Philippines: the key that unlocks the door to the Pacific.

General of the Army Douglas MacArthur
"Reminiscences"
McGraw-Hill Book Company, New York, 1964

Without sacrifice of the principles of justice the devious advances of international Communism must be firmly repelled as a threat to internal peace and the national security. To such end, so long as existing international tensions exist in Asia, adequate security forces should be maintained to safeguard Japan's internal peace against any threatened external attack.

Letter to Japanese Prime Minister,
August 20, 1951

Are we going to continue to permit the pressure of alien doctrines to strongly influence the orientation of foreign and domestic policy or regain trust in our own traditions, experience and free institutions and the wisdom of our own people.

Cleveland, Ohio,
September 6, 1951

Into the ensuing spiritual vacuum flowed the American concept of honor and justice and compassion drawn from our Christian teachings.

National Institute of Social Sciences
Annual Dinner,
Waldorf-Astoria Hotel, New York, New York,
November 8, 1951

For history teaches with unmistakable emphasis that appeasement but begets new and bloodier war.

U.S. Congress,
Washington, DC,
April 19, 1951

The magnificence of the courage and fortitude of the Korean people defies description. They have chosen to risk death rather than slavery. Their last words to me were "Don't scuttle the Pacific."

U.S. Congress,
Washington, DC,
April 19, 1951

Whatever the cause, the facts are undeniable. Our prestige abroad has reached a tragically low ebb and our leadership is little wanted.

Texas Legislature,
Austin, Texas,
June 13, 1951

We must finally come to realize that war is outmoded as an instrument of political policy, that it provides no solution for international problems; that it but threatens the participants with mutual national suicide.

Massachusetts Legislature,
Boston, Massachusetts,
July 25, 1951

You cannot control war; you can only abolish it.

Massachusetts Legislature,
Boston, Massachusetts,
July 25, 1951

Are we going to continue to permit the pressure of alien doctrines to strongly influence the orientation of foreign and domestic policy or regain trust in our own traditions, experience and free institutions and the wisdom of our own people?

Cleveland, Ohio,
September 6, 1951

At the birth of the Nation, Washington counseled strongly against our entering upon entangling alliances abroad lest we find ourselves involved in Europe's wars.

National Convention, The American Legion,
Miami, Florida,
October 17, 1951

The issue of war or peace is not based upon any sudden and unexpected change in the course of world events, or even direction of Soviet policy. Long before even the Second World War, the Soviet was known to plan suppression of the concept of freedom and the advance of Communism throughout the world, as rapidly as conditions would permit. We ourselves molded these conditions to the Soviet's plan by providing extraordinary facility for it to so deploy its military forces as to permit direct and decisive pressure upon many of the free nations of Europe and Asia.

National Convention,The American Legion,
Miami, Florida,
October 17, 1951

We must not again permit our leaders to gamble with the national security to serve political ends.

National Convention, The American Legion,
Miami, Florida,
October 17, 1951

We question the hasty plunging into foreign quarrels, instead of holding the country on a high moral plane as an impartial and just arbiter of international dissensions.

Opening, Centennial Celebration,
Seattle, Washington,
November 13, 1951

We dislike bombastic and provocative statements which settle nothing and but increase existing world tensions.

Opening, Centennial Celebration,
Seattle, Washington,
November 13, 1951

In the field of foreign policy, efforts are largely confined to the contribution of vast sums, which we do not have and must borrow, toward the rehabilitation of economies abroad, the rearming of other nations and the relief of foreign underprivileged and distressed. As a good neighbor we do desire to help the rest of the world in every reasonable way, but certainly that is no excuse either for the wrecking of our economy at home, or for covert encouragement of the terrible psychosis of war.

Joint Session, Mississippi Legislature,
Jackson, Mississippi,
March 22, 1952

Indeed, it would be immediately helpful if we but purged our foreign policy of imperialistic tendencies - not imperialistic in the sense that we covet the territory of others - but imperialistic in the pressure we bring to bear upon the purely domestic affairs of others. For this is an ear characterized by a universal sentiment of nationalism. This we must respect if we would gain the respect of others. The peoples of the world will only follow our leadership upon the basis of our moral integrity and spiritual as well as physical strength. They will measure us not by the monies we recklessly give them, but by the general attitudes with which we face the common problems of mankind.

Joint Session, Mississippi Legislature,
Jackson, Mississippi,
March 22, 1952

In one sector of the world, we oppose colonialism; in another, we support it.

Joint Session, Michigan Legislature,
Lansing, Michigan,
May 15, 1952

By what accomplishment may we justify the generous contribution we are making of our own material sustenance and the offer of the blood of our sons in support of the principle pf collective security in Western Europe, if not by the record in Korea?

Joint Session, Michigan Legislature,
Lansing, Michigan,
May 15, 1952

Everywhere the long arm of foreign influence dominates and controls even against our own national interests. Our will, our courage, our initiative, seem almost paralyzed.

Joint Session, Michigan Legislature,
Lansing, Michigan,
May 15, 1952

If I could voice but one solemn warning in the lengthening shadows of life, I would point to the jeopardy to our independence by the high-handed and reckless course of foreign-dominated national policy, and urge thoughtful reflection upon General Washington's stern and realistic order at another crisis in America's Past: "Let none but Americans stand guard tonight."

Joint Session, Michigan Legislature,
Lansing, Michigan,
May 15, 1952

Our ideal must be eventually the abolition of war.

Keynote Address,
Republic National Convention,
Chicago, Illinois,
July 7, 1952

We must fully understand that once we commit ourselves to the defense of others, the issue of war or peace is no longer in our exclusive hands, for we become but another pawn in the game of international power politics.

Keynote Address,
Republic National Convention,
Chicago, Illinois,
July 7, 1952

We must remain faithful to the commitments we have made to others, so long as they remain faithful to theirs made to us,...

Keynote Address,
Republic National Convention,
Chicago, Illinois,
July 7, 1952

While helping to the extent reasonably possible, we must not assume purely from altruism the risks and burdens which rightfully belong to others. We must abolish the idea that world leadership and universal respect may be purchased for a price. We must not hypothecate beyond redemption our own liberties in the illusory belief that the pledge of our resources will alone suffice to secure the liberties of others. They must help themselves even as we help them.

National Association of Manufacturers,
Waldorf-Astoria Hotel, New York, New York
December 5, 1952

All see the danger to our national integrity from yielding too much of our sovereign individualism.

National Association of Manufacturers,
Waldorf-Astoria Hotel, New York, New York
December 5, 1952

....nations are just as sensitive as are individuals; that nations recoil against arbitrary dictation by others just as do individuals; that nations lose their self-respect just as do individuals if the burdens they should bear themselves are borne by others; and that a nation's loss of self-respect more often than not is translated into antagonism against its benefactor just as is that of the individual.

National Association of Manufacturers,
Waldorf-Astoria Hotel, New York, New York
December 5, 1952

...weakness and vacillation of our foreign policy, is forcing us into isolation just as surely as though we deliberately set out to sever our foreign contacts.

National Association of Manufacturers,
Waldorf-Astoria Hotel, New York, New York
December 5, 1952

In foreign affairs our policies - or more truthfully our lack of policies - have been weak and vacillating and largely dictated from abroad.

Joint Session, Michigan Legislature,
Lansing, Michigan,
May 15, 1952

There should be no rivalry between our east and our west - no pitting of Atlantic interests against those of the Pacific. The problem is global, not sectional. The living standard of the peoples of the Oriental East must and will be raised to a closer relativity with that of the Occidental West.

Opening, Centennial Celebration,
Seattle, Washington,
November 13, 1951

(Ten days before the Korean War began) There is nothing in God's world more sure than this: Come what may, the United States is not going to scuttle in the Pacific.

From "Representative Speeches of General of
the Army Douglas MacArthur" compiled by the
Legislative Reference Service,
Library of Congress, ordered to be printed
April 29, 1964.

...may we, as victors, become architects of a new Japan....

Allied Control Council for Japan,
Tokyo, Japan,
April 5, 1946

In China, Generalissimo Chiang Kai-shek was gradually pushing the Communists back, being largely aided and supplied by the United States. ... Instead of pushing on to the victory that was within the Generalissimo's grasp, an armistice was arranged... After months of fruitless negotiation, he withdrew without tangible results, and the war for China resumed. But in this interval of seven months a decisive change had taken place. The Generalissimo had received no munitions or supplies from the United States, but the Soviets, working day and night, reinforced the Chinese Communist armies. ... They pressed their advantage to the fullest, and finally drove the Generalissimo's forces out of continental Asia onto Formosa. The decision to withhold previously pledged American support was one of the greatest mistakes ever made in our history. At one fell blow, everything that had been so laboriously built up since the days of John Hay was lost. It was the beginning of the crumbling of our power in continental Asia - the birth of the taunt, "Paper Tiger." Its consequences will be felt for centuries, and its ultimate disastrous effects on the fortunes of the free world are still to be unfolded.

General of the Army Douglas MacArthur
"Reminiscences"
McGraw-Hill Book Company, New York, 1964

Unquestionably the failure, through inertia, of our diplomacy to utilize the victory of Inchon as the basis for swift and dynamic action to restore peace and unity to Korea was one of the greatest contributing causes to the subsequent war initiated by Red China.

General of the Army Douglas MacArthur
"Reminiscences"
McGraw-Hill Book Company, New York, 1964

MacArthur Memorial in Norfolk, VA.

GOVERNMENT

Are we going to squander our limited resources to the point of our own inevitable exhaustion or adopt commonsense policies of frugality which will insure financial stability in our time and a worthwhile heritage in that of our progeny?

Cleveland, Ohio,
September 6, 1951

Are we going to continue to yield personal liberties and community autonomy to the steady and inexplorable centralization of all political power or restore the Republic to constitutional direction, regain our personal liberties and reassume the individual State's primary responsibility and authority in the conduct of local affairs?

Cleveland, Ohio,
September 6, 1951

Are we going to continue to permit the pressure of alien doctrines to strongly influence the orientation of foreign and domestic policy or regain trust in our own traditions, experience and free institutions and the wisdom of our own people.

Cleveland, Ohio,
September 6, 1951

In short, is American life of the future to be characterized by freedom or by servitude, strength or weakness. The answer must be clear and unequivocal if we are to avoid the pitfalls toward which we are heading with such certainty. In many respects it is not to be found in any dogma of political philosophy but in those immutable precepts which underlie the Ten Commandments.

Cleveland, Ohio,
September 6, 1951

To curb the growing tendency of political and military leaders to publicize for political advantage classified data concerning scientific developments incident to our military effort, and thus to yield the all important element of surprise.

National Convention, The American Legion,
Miami, Florida,
October 17, 1951

...to help preserve freedom for those who have the will and determination to do all in their power to defend their own freedom ...

National Convention, The American Legion,
Miami, Florida,
October 17, 1951

...avoid being drawn into unreasonable and unnecessary expenditures for armament to create an artificial domestic prosperity for political ends ...

National Convention, The American Legion,
Miami, Florida,
October 17, 1951

...avoid contributing the fruits of our system of free enterprise to support socialism or communism abroad under the spurious pretense that it serves our own military security;...

National Convention, The American Legion,
Miami, Florida,
October 17, 1951

...avoid aligning ourselves with colonial policies in Asia and the Middle East;...

National Convention, The American Legion,
Miami, Florida,
October 17, 1951

...avoid distributing our wealth for the purpose of buying the loyalty of others, or of sharing with others the wealth and security which we hold in sacred trust for our progeny ...

National Convention, The American Legion,
Miami, Florida,
October 17, 1951

For we find our western defense geared to an Island chain off the coast of continental Asia from which with air and sea supremacy we can dominate any predatory move threatening the Pacific Ocean area.

Opening, Centennial Celebration,
Seattle, Washington,
November 13, 1951

Such possibilities seem however beyond the comprehension of some high in our governmental circles who still feel that the Pacific coast marks the practical terminus of our advance and the westerly boundary of our immediate national interest - that any opportunity for the expansion of our foreign trade should be mainly in the area of Europe and the Middle East. Nothing could more surely put brake upon our growth as a strong and prosperous nation. Intentionally or not, it would yield to industrialized Europe the undisputed dominion over the trade and commerce of the Far East. More than this, it would in time surrender to European nations the moral, if not political, leadership of the Eastern hemisphere. Nothing could more clearly attest a marked recession from that far-sighted vision which animated the pioneer of one hundred years ago.

Opening, Centennial Celebration,
Seattle, Washington,
November 13, 1951

These pressures have already caused us to depart sharply from the course so long held toward national strength and moral greatness. Our economic stature built under the incentives of free enterprise is imperiled by our drift through the back door of confiscatory taxation toward State Socialism.

Opening, Centennial Celebration,
Seattle, Washington,
November 13, 1951

It (Socialism) discourages development of those moral forces which would preserve inviolate our representative form of government, answerable to the free will of the electorate.

Opening, Centennial Celebration,
Seattle, Washington,
November 13, 1951

Our country will (then) reassume that spiritual and moral leadership recently lost in a quagmire of political ineptitude and economic incompetence.

Opening, Centennial Celebration,
Seattle, Washington,
November 13, 1951

It is a singular habit in this country to raise high the military when war threatens, but to ignore security needs in the pleasanter times of peace.

General of the Army Douglas MacArthur
"Reminiscences"
McGraw-Hill Book Company, New York, 1964

...in war, there is no substitute for victory.

U. S. Military Academy,
West Point, New York,
May 12, 1962

...the soldier above all other people prays for peace, for he must suffer and bear the deepest wounds and scars of war.

U. S. Military Academy,
West Point, New York,
May 12, 1962

Plato quote: "Only the dead have seen the end of war."

U. S. Military Academy,
West Point, New York,
May 12, 1962

The foundation of our National Defense system is the Regular Army, and the foundation of the Regular Army is the officer. He is the soul of the system.

General of the Army Douglas MacArthur
"Reminiscences"
McGraw-Hill Book Company, New York, 1964

At first hand, I had seen what I thought were basic and fundamental weaknesses in prior forms of military occupations: the substitution of civil by military authority; the loss of self-respect and self-confidence by the people; ...

General of the Army Douglas MacArthur
"Reminiscences"
McGraw-Hill Book Company, New York, 1964

I shall stand with you for an America rededicated to those sacred and immutable ideals and concepts which guided our forefathers when drawing the design of American freedom.

Chicago, Illinois,
April 26, 1951

...diplomatic appeasement but sows the seeds of future conflicts.

Texas Legislature,
Austin, Texas,
June 13, 1951

My correspondence reflects a growing lack of faith by a large segment of our population in the responsibility and moral fiber of our own process of government.

Texas Legislature,
Austin, Texas,
June 13, 1951

The rights of individuals and communities have rapidly been curtailed in the advance toward central government.

Texas Legislature,
Austin, Texas,
June 13, 1951

Our prestige abroad has reached a tragically low ebb and our leadership is little wanted.

Texas Legislature,
Austin, Texas,
June 13, 1951

I am concerned over the moral degradation which will be ours in the aftermath of our failure fully and firmly to support the forces we have committed to battle in Korea, and to fulfill the obligation of protection we assumed when we accepted that unhappy nation's defense.

Texas Legislature,
Austin, Texas,
June 13, 1951

...propaganda is the primary instrument of totalitarian rule.

San Antonio, Texas,
June 15, 1951

For the drift away from our competitive system of free enterprise is threatening the initiative and incentive of our people...

Fort Worth, Texas,
June 16, 1951

This Nation's material wealth is built upon the vision and courage, the sweat and toil, hope and faith of our people.

Massachusetts Legislature,
Boston, Massachusetts,
July 25, 1951

...I find in existence a new and heretofore unknown and dangerous concept that the members of our armed forces owe primary allegiance and loyalty to those who temporarily exercise the authority of the executive branch of government, rather than to the country and its constitution which they are sworn to defend.

Massachusetts Legislature,
Boston, Massachusetts,
July 25, 1951

Public morality is the touchstone to the people's faith in the integrity of the governmental process.

Letter to Japanese Prime Minister,
August 20, 1951

Those who lack the enterprise, the vision and the courage to try a new approach when none others have succeeded fail completely the simple test of leadership.

Massachusetts Legislature,
Boston, Massachusetts,
July 25, 1951

The preservation, inviolate, of the economic system based upon free, private, competitive enterprise alone maximizes the initiative, the energy and in the end the productive capacity of the people.

Letter to Japanese Prime Minister,
August 20, 1951

The vigorous and faithful implementation of the existing land laws providing land ownership for agricultural workers and of the labor laws providing industrial workers a voice in the conditions of their employment is mandatory if these all-important segments of Japanese society are to enjoy their rightful dignity and opportunity, and social unrest based upon just grievance is to be avoided.

Letter to Japanese Prime Minister,
August 20, 1951

The Bill of Rights ordained by the Constitution must be vigilantly preserved if the government would be assured the people's full support. Public criticism should be encouraged rather than suppressed as providing a powerful check against the evils of mal-administration of the political power. Freedom of speech as an inalienable right should never e challenged unless it directly violates the laws governing libel and slander.

Letter to Japanese Prime Minister,
August 20, 1951

Both (domestic and foreign affairs) under the leadership now administering our government, have departed sharply from tradition and constitutional mandate.

National Convention, The American Legion,
Miami, Florida,
October 17, 1951

To give primary concern to our own security and the well-being of our people; to avoid distributing our wealth for the purpose of buying loyalty of others.

National Convention, The American Legion,
Miami, Florida,
October 17, 1951

Are we going to squander our limited resources to the point of our own inevitable exhaustion or adopt commonsense policies of frugality which will insure financial stability in our time and a worthwhile heritage in that of our progeny?

Are we going to continue to yield personal liberties and community autonomy to the steady and inexplorable centralization of all political power or restore the Republic to constitutional direction, regain our personal liberties and reassume the individual State's primary responsibility and authority in the conduct of local affairs?

Cleveland, Ohio,
September 6, 1951

To avoid aligning ourselves with colonial policies in Asia and the middle east;...

National Convention, The American Legion,
Miami, Florida,
October 17, 1951

To the early pioneer the Pacific coast marked the end of his courageous westerly advance - to us it should mark but the beginning. To him it delimited our western frontier - to us that frontier has been moved beyond the Pacific horizon.

Opening, Centennial Celebration,
Seattle, Washington,
November 13, 1951.

... we find our western defense geared to an Island chain off the coast of continental Asia from which with air and sea supremacy we can dominate any predatory move threatening the Pacific Ocean area.

Opening, Centennial Celebration,
Seattle, Washington,
November 13, 1951.

Such possibilities seem however beyond the comprehension of some high in our governmental circles who still feel that the Pacific coast marks the practical terminus of our advance and the westerly boundary of our immediate national interest - that any opportunity for the expansion of our foreign trade should be mainly in the area of Europe and the Middle East. Nothing could more surely put brake upon our growth as a strong and prosperous nation. Intentionally or not, it would yield to industrialized Europe the undisputed dominion over the trade and commerce of the Far East. More than this, it would in time surrender to European nations the moral, if not political, leadership of the Eastern hemisphere. Nothing could more clearly attest a marked recession from that far-sighted vision which animated the pioneer of one hundred years ago.

Opening, Centennial Celebration,
Seattle, Washington,
November 13, 1951.

These pressures have already caused us to depart sharply from the course so long held toward national strength and moral greatness. Our economic stature built under the incentives of free enterprise is imperiled by our drift through the back door of confiscatory taxation toward State Socialism.

Opening, Centennial Celebration,
Seattle, Washington,
November 13, 1951.

Our political stature built upon wise and self-effacing statesmanship and sound domestic policy, has been sadly impaired by a succession of diplomatic blunders abroad and reckless spendthrift aims at home.

Opening, Centennial Celebration,
Seattle, Washington,
November 13, 1951.

I stand on this rostrum with a sense of deep humility and great pride - humility in the wake of those great American architects of our history who have stood here before me, pride in the reflection that this forum of legislative debate represents human liberty in the purest form yet devised. Here are centered the hopes and aspirations and faith of the entire human race.

U. S. Congress,
Washington, DC,
April 19, 1951

I do not stand here as advocate for any partisan cause for the issues are fundamental and reach quite beyond the realm of partisan consideration. They must be resolved on the highest plane of national interest if our course is to prove sound and our future protected.

U. S. Congress,
Washington, DC,
April 19, 1951

I address you with neither rancor nor bitterness in the fading twilight of life with but one purpose in mind - to serve my country.

U. S. Congress,
Washington, DC,
April 19, 1951

The issues are global and so interlocked that to consider the problems of one sector, oblivious to those of another, is but to court disaster for the whole.

U. S. Congress,
Washington, DC,
April 19, 1951

While Asia is commonly referred to as the gateway to Europe, it is no less true that Europe is the gateway to Asia. And the broad influence of the one cannot fail to have its impact upon the other.

U. S. Congress,
Washington, DC,
April 19, 1951

...with little opportunity to achieve any degree of social justice, individual dignity or a higher standard of life such as guided our own noble administration of the Philippines, the peoples of Asia found their opportunity in the war just past to throw off the shackles of colonialism and now see the dawn of new opportunity, a heretofore unfelt dignity and the self-respect of political freedom.

U. S. Congress,
Washington, DC,
April 19, 1951

...the Asian peoples covet the right to shape their own free destiny.

U. S. Congress,
Washington, DC,
April 19, 1951

What the (Asian) peoples strive for is the opportunity for a little more food in their stomachs, a little better clothing on their backs, a little firmer roof over their heads, and the realization of the normal nationalist urge for political freedom.

U. S. Congress,
Washington, DC,
April 19, 1951

The Japanese people since the war have undergone the greatest reformation recorded in modern history. With a commendable will, eagerness to learn and marked capacity to understand, they have, from the ashes left in war's wake, erected in Japan an edifice dedicated to the primacy of individual liberty and personal dignity, and in the ensuing process thee has been created a truly representative government committed to the advance of political morality, freedom of economic enterprise, and social justice.

U. S. Congress,
Washington, DC,
April 19, 1951

Politically, economically and socially, Japan is now abreast of many free nations of the earth and will not again fail the universal trust.

U. S. Congress,
Washington, DC,
April 19, 1951

Of our former ward, the Philippines, we can look forward in confidence that the existing unrest will be corrected and a strong and healthy nation will grow in the longer aftermath of war's terrible destructiveness. We must be patient and understanding and never fail them, as in our hour of need they did not fail us.

U. S. Congress,
Washington, DC,
April 19, 1951

Apart from the military need as I saw it, to neutralize the sanctuary protection given the enemy north of the Yalu, I felt that military necessity in the conduct of the war made mandatory:

1. The intensification of our economic blockage against China;

2. The imposition of a naval blockade against the China coast;

3. Removal of restrictions on air reconnaissance of China's coastal areas and of Manchuria;

4. Removal of restrictions on the forces of the Republic of China on Formosa with logistical support to contribute to their effective operations against the common enemy.

For entertaining these views, all professionally designed to support our forces committed to Korea and bring hostilities to an end with the least possible delay and at a saving of countless American and Allied lives, I have been severely criticized in lay circles, principally abroad, despite my understanding that from a military standpoint the above views have been fully shared in past by practically every military leader concerned with the Korean campaign, including our own Joint Chiefs of Staff.

U. S. Congress,
Washington, DC,
April 19, 1951

Government has assumed progressively the arrogant mantle of oligarchic power as the great moral and ethical principles upon which our nation grew strong have been discarded or remolded to serve narrow political purposes. The cost of government has become so great and the consequent burden of taxation so heavy that the system of free enterprise which built our great material strength has become imperiled.

The rights of individuals and communities have rapidly been curtailed in the advance toward centralized power and the spiritual and material strength, amassed through our original concept of a federation - erected upon the local responsibility and autonomy of its several components - shows marked deterioration.

Possibly these adverse factors account for our inability to advance a vigorous and courageous leadership at a time when the world never more needed such a leadership.

Texas Legislature,
Austin, Texas,
June 13, 1951

There are those who seek to subvert government from being the guardian of the people's rights, to make of it an instrument of despotic power.

Flag Day,
Houston, Texas,
June 14, 1951

There are those who seek to make the burden of taxation so great and the progressive increase so alarming that the spirit of adventure, tireless energy and masterful initiative which built the material strength of the nation shall become stultified and inert.

Flag Day,
Houston, Texas,
June 14, 1951

MacArthur in his usual pose surrounded by his staff and military admirers, August, 1945.

Before the descendants of these early American patriots I am honored, indeed, to address this legislative assembly in response to its thoughtful and kind invitation. I do so with neither partisan affiliation nor political purpose. But I have been warned by many that an outspoken course, even if it be solely of truth, will bring down upon my head ruthless retaliation - that efforts will be made to destroy public faith in the integrity of my views - not by force of just argument but by the application of the false methods of propaganda. I am told in effect I must follow blindly the leader - keep silent - or take the bitter consequences. I had thought Abraham Lincoln had pinned down for all time this ugly code when he declared: "To sin by silence when they should protest makes cowards of men." I shall raise my voice as loud and as often as I believe it to be in the interest of the American people. I shall dedicate all of my energies to restoring to American life those immutable principles and ideals which your forebears and mine handed down to us in sacred trust. I shall assist in the regaining of that moral base for both public and private life which will restore the people's faith in the integrity of public institutions and the private faith of ever man in the integrity of his neighbor. I shall set my course to the end that no man need fear to speak the truth. I could not do less, for the opportunities for service my country has given me and the honors it has conferred upon me have imposed an obligation which is not discharged by the termination of public service.

Massachusetts Legislature,
Boston, Massachusetts,
July 25, 1951

This nation's material wealth is built upon the vision and courage, the sweat and toil, hope and faith of our people. There has been no magic involved upon which we might again call to replenish our denuded coffers. We can either advance upon the security of sound principles or we can plunge on to the precipice of disaster toward which we are now headed in the dangerous illusion that our wealth is inexhaustible - and can therefore be limitlessly shared with others.

Massachusetts Legislature,
Boston, Massachusetts,
July 25, 1951

The survival of the free world is infinitely more dependent upon the maintenance of a strong, vigorous, healthy and independent America as a leavening influence than upon any financial aid which we might provide under our own existing stringencies.

Massachusetts Legislature,
Boston, Massachusetts,
July 25, 1951

The free world's one great hope for survival now rests upon the maintaining and preserving of our own strength.

Massachusetts Legislature,
Boston, Massachusetts,
July 25, 1951

We stand today at a critical moment in history - at a vital crossroad. In one direction is the path of courageous patriots seeking in humility but the opportunity to serve their country; the other that of those selfishly seeking to entrench autocratic power.

The one group stands for implacable resistance against Communism; the other for compromising with Communism. The one stands for our traditional system of government and freedom; the other for a socialist state and slavery.

The one boldly speaks the truth; the other spreads propaganda, fear and deception. The one denounces excessive taxation, bureaucratic government and corruption; the other seeks more taxes, more bureaucratic power, and shields corruption.

The people, as the ultimate rulers, must choose the course our nation shall follow. On their decision rests the future of our free civilization and the survival of our Christian faith.

> *Massachusetts Legislature,*
> *Boston, Massachusetts,*
> *July 25, 1951*

Our trip to this great state has been an inspiring one for here was born the concept of American Liberty...

> *Springfield, Massachusetts,*
> *July 26, 1951*

Restraint and frugality in the use of the public purse produces economic stability, encourages individual thrift and minimizes the burden of taxation.

> *Letter to the Prime Minister of Japan,*
> *August 20, 1951*

The preservation, inviolate, of the economic system based upon free, private, competitive enterprise alone maximizes the initiative, the energy and in the end the productive capacity of the people.

> *Letter to the Prime Minister of Japan,*
> *August 20, 1951*

MacArthur with other commanders assemble at Alamo HQ, December 1943.

Since my return from service abroad I have enjoyed the privilege, the freedom and the opportunities of private citizenship. I have seen many new and wonderful things but some which to me create a disturbing outlook for the future. Possibly one of the most pernicious is our steady drift toward totalitarian rule with the suppression of those personal liberties which have formed the foundation stones to our political, economic and social advance to national greatness.

Our government now differs substantially from the design of our forefathers as laid down in the Constitution. They envisaged a federation of sovereign states with only such limited power resting in the federal authority as became necessary to serve the common interests of all.

But under the stress of national emergencies during the past two decades, there has been a persistent and progressive centralization of power in the Federal Government with only superficial restoration to the States and the people as emergencies subsided. This drift has resulted in an increasingly dangerous paternalistic relationship between Federal Government and private citizen, with the mushrooming of agency after agency designed to control the individual.

Authority specifically reserved to the States by constitutional mandate has been ignored in the ravenous effort to further centralize the political power. Within the Federal Government itself there has been a further and dangerous centralization.

For example, the Department of State, originally established for the sole purpose of the conduct of foreign diplomacy, has become in effect a general operating agency of government, exercising authority and influence over many facets of executive administration formerly reserved to the President or the heads of other departments. The Department of State indeed is rapidly assuming the character of a Prime Ministry, notwithstanding that its Secretary is an appointed official, neither chosen by nor answerable directly to the people.

This drift toward totalitarian rule is reflected not only in this shift toward centralized power, but as well in the violent manner in which exception is taken to the citizen's voice when raised in criticism of those who exercise the political power.

There seems to be an determination to suppress individual voice and opinion, which can only be regarded as symptomatic of the beginning of a general trend toward mass thought control. Abusive language and arbitrary action, rather than calm, dispassionate and just argument, ill becomes the leadership of a great nation conceived in liberty and dedicated to a course of morality and justice. It challenges the concept of free speech and is an attempt at direct suppression through intimidation of that most vital check against the abuse of political power - public criticism.

If long countenanced by free men, it can but lead to those controls upon conviction and conscience which traditionally have formed stepping stones to dictatorial power.

Cleveland, Ohio,
September 6, 1951

Are we going to squander our limited resources to the point of our own inevitable exhaustion or adopt common sense policies of frugality which will insure financial stability in our time and a worthwhile heritage in that of our progeny?

Cleveland, Ohio,
September 6, 1951

I recall so vividly the American Legion's warning to the country at the close of the war some six years ago. Its resolution read as follows: "...the only present guarantee of our nation's safety and freedom and the best presently available assurance of world peace is to have in the hands of this great peace-loving nation the mightiest armament in the world."

National Convention, The American Legion,
Miami, Florida,
October 17, 1951

I have been especially stirred by your reference to my role in the erection of New Japan upon the ashes left in the wake of war's destructive violence. Never in history has a nation and its people been more completely crushed than were the Japanese at the end of the struggle. They had suffered more than a military debacle more than the destruction of their armed forces, more than the elimination of their industrial bases, more even than the occupation of their land by foreign bayonets. Their entire faith in the Japanese way of life, cherished as invincible for many centuries, perished in the agony of their total defeat. Into the ensuing spiritual vacuum flowed the American concept of honor and justice and compassion drawn from our Christian teachings. It was received with eagerness, and as understanding of its true meaning came to the Japanese mind, with growing reverence and devotion. Thus was born the new Japan.

National Institute of Social Sciences
Annual Dinner,
Waldorf-Astoria Hotel, New York, New York,
November 8, 1951

Our economic stature built under the incentives of free enterprise is imperiled by our drift through the back door of confiscatory taxation toward State Socialism.

Opening, Centennial Celebration,
Seattle, Washington,
November 13, 1951

Our country is facing one of the grave crises in American history - not so much from external threat, although the forces of evil which our own political and military blunders have helped so much to build, must by no means be ignored - but from internal pressures which threaten the very survival of our liberties. These pressures have already made sharp inroads into our free way of life and impaired much of the incentive which has encouraged development of those basic virtues and traits of character from which has emerged our traditional American initiative, American energy and that indomitable American will which in past has preserved our moral balance and produced our material strength.

Article, American Legion Magazine,
January, 1952

The very character of our nation is molded from those noblest of human virtues - faith, hope and charity. But it is a well-tested good rule to let first things be first. Let us regain faith and hope in our ability to achieve our own free destiny and let charity begin at home. Let us concern ourselves first with our own underprivileged and distressed before we take further from the little they have. The will to be free either exists in the human heart or all the money in the world cannot put it there.

Thus, despite the billions we have poured abroad, I doubt that we have gained a single communist convert to the cause of human freedom or inspired new or deeper friendships. And, as quite obviously, the people of Western Europe do not generally share with our own leaders the fear of Soviet military designs, despite these billions we seem to have made little progress in convincing them that they themselves should vigorously act to shore up their own defenses. We hear no clamor to pledge their own lives, their own fortunes and their own sacred honor ind defense of their own liberties.

Mississippi Legislature,
Jackson, Mississippi,
March 22, 1952

Our world leadership may only be regained if we ourselves are strong - spiritually as well as physically - and have the moral courage and the vision to advance constructive ideas with the will ourselves to see them through.

Mississippi Legislature,
Jackson, Mississippi,
March 22, 1952

(Voices in opposition) even contend that my advocacy of a return of this Nation to constitutional direction, of a restoration of those noble and well-tested principles and ideals which we were formerly so proud to call American tradition, of a revitalization of the moral fiber which once commanded full faith in our public institutions, is merely the pleasing of partisan politics - that it renders mine the voice of a biased politician.

Michigan Legislature,
Lansing, Michigan,
May 15, 1952

Government has indeed become complex, but is largely a self-induced complexity. It springs from its increasingly arbitrary nature and the labyrinth of governmental agencies created in the endless effort toward centralization and the imposition of new and expanding Federal controls upon community and citizen.

Michigan Legislature,
Lansing, Michigan,
May 15, 1952

We would regain the Jeffersonian standard that the least government is easily the best government.

Michigan Legislature,
Lansing, Michigan,
May 15, 1952

Restore simplicity in public administration and you will at once not only drastically reduce the financial burden upon the people, but you will raise the standard of individual life and regain the level of community and personal dignity.

Michigan Legislature,
Lansing, Michigan,
May 15, 1952

As Lincoln once said, "If this nation is ever destroyed, it will be from within, not from without."

Michigan Legislature,
Lansing, Michigan,
May 15, 1952

We must not underestimate the peril. It must not be brushed off lightly. It must not be scoffed at as our present leadership has been prone to do by hurling childish epithets, such as "red herring," "character assassin," "scandal monger," "witch hunt," "political gagster," and like vulgar terms designed to confuse or conceal the real issues and intimidate those who, recognizing the gravity of the danger, would expose it to the light of public scrutiny and understanding, For it is upon the shaking foundation stones of a complacent citizenry that minority pressures become controlling forces and liberty yields to tyranny.

Michigan Legislature,
Lansing, Michigan,
May 15, 1952

We must preserve and conserve our industrial potential to counter any major threat against the general peace, with the invincible determination to meet any force hurled at us with adequate counter force.

Michigan Legislature,
Lansing, Michigan,
May 15, 1952

It is now even proposed that our two-party political system be abandoned for all practical purposes and that both parties unite under the leadership of the same individual. Could there be a more shocking proposal?

Michigan Legislature,
Lansing, Michigan,
May 15, 1952

The history of the world shows that republics and democracies have generally lost their liberties by way of passing from civilian to a quasi-military status. Nothing is more conducive to arbitrary rule than the military junta. It would be a tragic development indeed if this generation was forced to look to the rigidity of military dominance and discipline to redeem it from the tragic failure of a civilian administration. It might well destroy our historic and wise concept which holds to the supremacy of the civil power.

Michigan Legislature,
Lansing, Michigan,
May 15, 1952

From the acknowledged leadership of the world six years ago, we have drifted into an equivocal position in which our main influence seems to be confined to that of paymaster.

Michigan Legislature,
Lansing, Michigan,
May 15, 1952

This harmony among individuals could apply with no less force among nations, if the leaders of the world would so permit.

City Hall,
Detroit, Michigan,
May 16, 1952

Both in labor and in industry, this calls for a high level of statesmanship dedicated to the common purpose of advancing a liberal and unexploited labor movement and an industrial economy sufficiently free from government controls to maintain a reasonable profit potential.

City Hall,
Detroit, Michigan,
May 16, 1952

To such end they have sought to circumvent the safeguards to our liberties wisely written into the Constitution of the United States. At one stage there was even the attempt to subvert the independence of our Supreme Court by adding new members pliable to the will of the executive - at another, the claim of extraordinary "inherent" power without the slightest sanction in law.

Keynote Address,
Republic National Convention,
Chicago, Illinois,
July 7, 1952

Spiritually and physically we posses the resource, properly conserved and realistically applied, to lead toward a world freed from the exhausting wars which have so plagued the past. This is a practical purpose, not visionary. For the destructiveness of modern war has now in the atomic age become too frightful to contemplate by even a potential victor.

Keynote Address,
Republic National Convention,
Chicago, Illinois,
July 7, 1952

Most officials of our government over the past years will deny, and justifiably, any intent to establish in this nation the basis for the emergence of a Socialistic or even eventually a Communistic state, but the course of fiscal policy has done just that.

The fact is unmistakable and clear that if the capitalistic system - free enterprise - is to be preserved to the future generations of our people, the course of government must now be sharply reoriented and America's industrial leadership must assume an invincible and uncompromising defense of that system.

National Association of Manufacturers,
Waldorf-Astoria Hotel, New York, New York,
December 5, 1952

...reach into the future yet never neglect the past.

U. S. Military Academy,
West Point, New York,
May 12, 1962

It (deep spiritual urge) is an infallible reminder that our greatest hope and faith rests upon two mighty symbols - the Cross and the Flag.

Flag Day,
Houston, Texas,
June 14, 1951

What, I have been asked, is our greatest internal menace? If I were permitted but one sentence of reply, but one phrase of warning, it would be - end invisible government based upon propaganda and restore truly representative government based on truth.

San Antonio, Texas,
June 15, 1951

I called for reinforcements, but was informed that reinforcements were not available. I made clear that if not permitted to destroy the enemy build-up bases north of the Yalu; if not permitted to utilize the friendly Chinese force of some six hundred thousand men on Formosa; if not permitted to blockade the China coast to prevent the Chinese Reds from getting succor from without; and if there were to be no hope of major reinforcements, the position of the command from the military standpoint forbade victory. We could hold in Korea by constant maneuver and at an approximate area where our supply line advantages were in balance with the supply line disadvantages of the enemy, but we could hope at best for only an indecisive campaign, with its terrible and constant attrition upon our forces if the enemy utilized his full military potential. I have constantly called for the new political decisions essential to a solution. Efforts have been made to distort my position. It has been said that I was in effect a warmonger. Nothing could be further from the truth. I know war as few other men now living know it, and nothing to me is more revolting. I have long advocated its complete abolition as its very destructiveness on both friend and foe has rendered it useless as a means of settling international disputes. Indeed, on the 2nd of September 1945, just following the surrender of the Japanese nation on the battleship Missouri, I formally cautioned as follows:

"Men since the beginning of time have sought peace. Various methods through the ages have been attempted to devise international process to prevent or settle disputes between nations. From the very start, workable methods were found insofar as individual citizens were concerned, but the mechanics of an instrumentality of larger international scope have never been successful. Military alliances, balances of power, Leagues of Nations, all in turn failed, leaving the only path to be by way of the crucible of war. The utter destructiveness of war now blots out this alternative. We have had our last chance. If we will not devise some greater and more equitable system, Armageddon will be at our door. The problem basically is theological and involved a spiritual recrudescence and improvement of human character that will synchronize with our almost matchless advances in science, art, literature and all material and cultural developments of the past two thousand years. It must be of the spirit if we are to save the flesh."

But once war is forced upon us, there is no other alternative than to apply every available means to bring it to a swift end. War's very object is victory - not prolonged indecision. In war, indeed, there can be no substitute for victory.

There are some who for varying reasons would appease Red China. They are blind to history's clear lesson. For history teaches with unmistakable emphasis that appeasement but begets new and bloodier war. It points to no single instance where the end has justified that means - where appeasement has led to more than a sham peace. Like blackmail, it lays the basis for new and successively greater demands, until, as in blackmail, violence becomes the only other alternative. Why, my soldiers asked of me, surrender military advantages to an enemy in the field? I could not answer. Some may say to avoid spread of the conflict into an all-out war with China; others, to avoid Soviet intervention. Neither explanation seems valid. For China is already engaging with the maximum power it can commit and the Soviet will not necessarily mesh its actions with our moves. Like a cobra, any new enemy will more likely strike whenever it feels that the relativity in military or other potential is in its favor on a worldwide basis.

U. S. Congress,
Washington, DC,
April 19, 1951

At war's end the main agency for maintaining the peace became the United Nations. This organization was conceived in a common desire that the scourge of war should not again be visited upon the earth. It was dedicated to the principle that all mankind of unalienable right should live in justice and liberty and peace.

It represents perhaps the noblest effort man has yet made to evolve a universal code based upon the highest of moral precepts. It became the keystone to an arch of universal hope.

Yet in practice its efforts become increasingly doubtful of ultimate success. Its organization is inherently weak, legislatively, judicially and executively. It lacks legislative strength because its members, not being elected but merely appointed, are not answerable directly to the people. It lacks judicial strength because there is no accepted international code of sufficient moral authority or purpose to mold and guide its decisions. It lacks executive strength because it controls no agencies of sufficient power to enforce its mandates.

It threatens to fail; if the innate selfishness of its members does not yield to universal needs; if the mechanics of its operations are not corrected to prevent the will of one nation from counterbalancing the collective will of the others; if it does not stop obstructionist tactics, even by expulsion if necessary, of its own unruly members; if regional military alliances must be organized within its membership to undertake collective security measures against threat from other members; if it allows itself to be reduced to a mere forum for meaningless and acrimonious debate, and a springboard for propaganda.

Unless a strong and dynamic sense of responsibility emerges within its ranks capable of rallying the forces of good throughout the world; of establishing a higher moral tone to its deliberations and activities; of correcting its existing institutional and mechanical weaknesses, the United Nations may well go the way of its predecessor League and perish as a force to guide civilization.

But the great moral and spiritual purpose which animated its formation - the abolition of war from the face of the earth - will always live and a way must be found to achieve that purpose. This way cannot be found, however, if nations are so blind as not to see their own weaknesses - so weak as not to correct them.

Cleveland, Ohio,
September 6, 1951

Men since the beginning of time have sought peace. Various methods through the ages have been attempted to devise an international process to prevent or settle disputes between nations. From the very start, workable methods were found insofar as individual citizens were concerned, but the mechanics of an instrumentality of larger international scope have never been successful. Military alliances, balance of power, leagues of nations, all in turn failed, leaving the only path to be by way of the crucible of war. The utter destructiveness of war now blots out this alternative. We have had our last chance. If we will not devise some greater and more equitable system. Armageddon will be at our door. The problem basically is theological and involves a spiritual recrudescence and improvement of human character that will synchronize with our almost matchless advances in science, art, literature, and all material and cultural developments of the past 2,000 years. It must be of the spirit if we are to save the flesh.

VJ Day Broadcast, U.S.S. Missouri,
September 2, 1945

While we must be prepared to meet the trial of war if war comes, we should gear our foreign and domestic policies toward the ultimate goal - the abolition of war from the face of the earth.

That is what practically all mankind - all the great masses which populate the world - long and pray for. Therein lies the road, the only road, to universal peace and prosperity.

Massachusetts Legislature,
Boston, Massachusetts,
July 25, 1951

The voice of the people must be heeded... The implacable guide must be faith in those immutable principles and ideals which give spiritual strength to our Constitution.

There must be reflected that degree of humility which recognizes the religious base upon which our nation was founded, with an indomitable determination to preserve it. The threat to freedom in peace is no less sinister than in war. Our country's future must not go by default.

National Convention, The American Legion,
Miami, Florida,
October 17, 1951

It should be inconceivable that our leaders would close their eyes to any direction of opportunity - to concentrate upon any one avenue to the exclusion of any other. In the pioneering spirit, it should be our undeviating purpose to develop the maximum of global trade, ignoring only those unfriendly areas and peoples which our trade would assist in bringing abusive pressure against us.

Opening, Centennial Celebration,
Seattle, Washington,
November 13, 1951

...the course is clear. There must be such a development of opportunity that the requirements for a better life in the Oriental East may be filled from the almost unlimited industrial potential of the Occidental West. The human and material resources of the East would be used in compensation for the manufactures of the West.

Once this elementary logic is recognized, trade with the Far East may be expected rapidly to expand under the stimulus of American vision, American enterprise and American pioneering spirit. The pioneer of the 20th Century has in all respects as broad an avenue of advance as did the pioneer of the 19th Century...

In the face of such future opportunities, any concept of "scuttling" in the Pacific would be a direct negation of the spirit of our pioneer forefathers who stopped at no river, at no mountain, at no natural barrier in their driving urge to open the West. It is indulged in only by thee who lack the vision to comprehend and assess the full significance of global potentialities and who lack the moral courage to take maximum advantage of them.

Opening, Centennial Celebration,
Seattle, Washington,
November 13, 1951

Trade with Asia has historically been largely a European monopoly, protected by colonial ties. This monopoly was broken with the demise of colonial rule at war's end and must never be restored.

Opening, Centennial Celebration,
Seattle, Washington,
November 13, 1951

The Japanese people since the war have undergone the greatest reformation recorded in modern history. With a commendable will, eagerness to learn, and marked capacity to understand, they have, from the ashes left in war's wake, erected in Japan an edifice dedicated to the primacy of individual liberty and personal dignity, and in the ensuing process there has been created a truly representative government committed to the advance of political morality, freedom of economic enterprise, and social justice. Politically, economically and socially Japan is now abreast of many free nations of the earth and will not again fail the universal trust.

U. S. Congress,
Washington, DC,
April 19, 1951

In the Pacific we and our friends maintain an island defense chain off the coast of continental Asia which must be preserved inviolate at any cost.

Despite some public statements to the contrary, there is reason to fear that it is still the over-riding purpose of some of our political leaders, under the influence of allies who maintain diplomatic ties with Communist China, to yield the Island of Formosa at an opportune time to the Chinese henchmen of international Communism.

The effect of such action would be to breach our island defense chain, threaten peace on the Pacific and ultimately endanger the security of our Pacific coastal area.

There is little doubt that the yielding of Formosa and the seating of Communist China in the United Nations was fully planned when I called upon the enemy commander in Korea on March 24 to meet me in the field to arrange armistice terms. This I did in view of the fundamental weakness of his military position due to the lack of industrial base in China capable of supporting modern warfare.

The opposition I expressed to yielding Formosa and seating Red China, with the overwhelming support it received from the American people, unquestionably wrecked the secret plan to yield on these issues as the price for peace in Korea. There followed the violent Washington reaction in personal retaliation against me for what was actually so normal a military move.

National Convention, The American Legion,
Miami, Florida,
October 17, 1951

The tragedy is that since the advent of the war with Red China there has been no definition of the political policy which would provide a solution for the new problems thereby created. This has resulted in a policy vacuum heretofore unknown to war.

However great the effort to distract attention from the main issues by introducing into public discussion extraneous and irrelevant matters, the fundamental question still remains the same - what is the policy for Korea?

Chicago, Illinois,
April 26, 1951

The tragedy of Korea is further heightened by the fact that as military action is confined to its territorial limits, it condemns that nation, which it is our purpose to save, to suffer the devastating impact of full naval and air bombardment, while the enemy's sanctuaries are fully protected from such attack and devastation. Of the nations of the world, Korea alone, up to now, is the sole one which has risked its all against Communism.

The magnificence of the courage and fortitude of the Korean people defies description. They have chosen to risk death rather than slavery.

U. S. Congress,
Washington, DC,
April 19, 1951

I have been amazed, and deeply concerned, since my return, to observe the extent to which the orientation of our national policy tends to depart from the traditional courage, vision and forthrightness which has animated and guided our great leaders of the past, to be now largely influenced, if not indeed in some instances dictated from abroad and dominated by fear of what others may think or others may do.

Never before in our history can precedent be found for such a subordination of policy to the opinions of others with a minimum regard for the direction of our own national interest. Never before have we geared national policy to timidity and fear.

The guide, instead, has invariably been one of high moral principle and the courage to decide great issues on the spiritual level of what is right and what is wrong. Yet, in Korea today, we have reached that degree of moral trepidation that we pay tribute in the blood of our sons to the doubtful belief that the hand of a blustering potential enemy may in some way be thus stayed.

Texas Legislature,
Austin, Texas,
June 13, 1951

The national administration came under a control characterized by narrow vision and overriding personal ambition. The power of government was used as a political leverage to obtain more and greater centralization of authority. Political greed became the dominant factor in government and the fortunes of the political party of the administration began to receive primary consideration over and above the public interest.

Laws and clearly defined precedents wich obstructed this concentration of power were brushed aside and the democracy of representative government began to yield to the concept of governmental autocracy.

In the ensuing movement toward the ascendancy of men over laws, the meaning and intent of the Constitution became rapidly corrupted.

Mississippi Legislature,
Jackson, Mississippi,
March 22, 1952

There are those who plan to alter the constitutional checks and balances established to preserve the integrity of our coordinate branches. There are those who seek to make the burden of taxation so great and the progressive increase so alarming that the spirit of adventure, tireless energy and masterful initiative which built the material strength of the nation shall become stultified and inert. There are those who seek to make all men servants of the State. There are those who seek to change our system of free enterprise which, whatever its faults, commands the maximum of energy and human resource and provides the maximum of benefits in human happiness and contentment.

Flag Day,
Houston, Texas,
June 14, 1951

Government has assumed progressively the arrogant mantle of oligarchic power, as the great moral and ethical principles upon which our Nation grew strong have been discarded or remolded to serve narrow political purposes.

Texas Legislature,
Austin, Texas,
June 13, 1951

There are other disturbing signs that some of the peoples we seek to bolster are showing a lack of will to muster their own full resource in their own defense. There appear to be many among them who feel that their defense is and should be our sole responsibility and that beyond a token military collaboration they should confine their own energy and resource to the building of their civilian economy - some indeed who go so far as to advocate that money appropriated by our Congress for their military defense would be diverted to civilian purpose.

The startling thing is that such viewpoints are not lacking in support among our own leaders. Apparently some of them, more in line with Marxian philosophy than animated by a desire to preserve freedom, would finance the defense of others as a means of sharing with them our wealth.

This wealth, accumulated by our own initiative and industry under the incentives of free enterprise, would then serve as the means of covering socialist or communist deficits abroad. The ultimate effect, whatever the intent, would be to reduce our own standard of life to a level of universal mediocrity.

National Convention, The American Legion,
Miami, Florida,
October 17, 1951

Our leaders must throw off the complacent belief that the only threat to our survival is from without. All freedoms lost since war's end have been and result of internal pressures rather than external assault.

National Convention, The American Legion,
Miami, Florida,
October 17, 1951

Our government now differs substantially from the design of our forefathers as laid down in the Constitution. They envisaged a federation of sovereign states with only such limited power resting in the federal authority as became necessary to serve the common interests of all.

But under the stress of national emergencies during the past two decades, there has been a persistent and progressive centralization of power in the Federal Government with only superficial restoration to the States and the people as emergencies subsided.

This drift has resulted in an increasingly dangerous paternalistic relationship between Federal Government and private citizen, with the mushrooming of agency after agency designed to control the individual.

Authority specifically reserved to the States by constitutional mandate has been ignored in the ravenous effort to further centralize the political power.

Cleveland, Ohio,
September 6, 1951

Within the Federal Government itself there has been a further and dangerous centralization. For example, the Department of State, originally established for the sole purpose of the conduct of foreign diplomacy, has become in effect a general operating agency of government, exercising authority and influence over many facets of executive administration formerly reserved to the President or the heads of other departments. The Department of State indeed is rapidly assuming the character of a Prime Ministry, notwithstanding that its Secretary is an appointed official, neither chosen by nor answerable directly to the people.

This drift toward totalitarian rule is reflected not only in this shift toward centralized power, but as well in the violent manner in which exception is taken to the citizen's voice when raised in criticism of those who exercise the political power.

There seems to be a determination to suppress individual voice and opinion, which can only be regarded as symptomatic of the beginning of a general trend toward mass thought control. Abusive language and arbitrary action, rather than calm dispassionate and just argument, ill becomes the leadership of a great nation conceived in liberty and dedicated to a course of morality and justice.

Cleveland, Ohio,
September 6, 1951

These pressures (internal pressures now at work to weaken that heritage of America's past) have already caused us to depart sharply from the course so long held toward national strength and moral greatness.

Our economic stature built under the incentives of free enterprise is imperiled by our drift through the back door of confiscatory taxation toward State Socialism.

Opening, Centennial Celebration,
Seattle, Washington,
November 13, 1951

Major General Bertrandais with Japanese officials, August, 1945.

Therein lies the blueprint to a Socialist State. Therein lies the great issue now before our people - shall we preserve our freedom, or yield it to a centralized government under the concept of Socialism. There can be no compromise. It must be all or nothing; the traditional American way of life, or a totalitarian concept imported from abroad. All other issues are but secondary to this one which strikes at the very roots of our personal liberties and representative form of government.

For Socialism, once a reality, destroys that moral fiber which is the creation of freedom. It breeds every device which produced totalitarian role.

It is true that our Constitution established checks and balances designed to safeguard against such dangers, but such safeguard is ignored by those who seek to entrench personal political power through preferential treatment for some at the general expense of all. This carnival of special privilege cannot fail to undermine our heritage of character. It discourages development of those moral forces which would preserve inviolate our representative form of government, answerable to the free will of the electorate.

The great bulwark of the Republic, individual and collective self-reliance, is under constant threat through a carefully designed and progressive paternalism which renders both community and individual increasingly dependent upon the support of the Federal Government. In all areas of private welfare, the Socialist planners seek to inject the Federal hand to produce a progressive weakening of the structure of individual character.

The area of possible resistance to this creeping sabotage of freedom is being constantly narrowed as the Federal Government arrogates to itself more and more of the remaining tax potential. ... Should this trend continue, the Federal Government may well become for all practical purposes the sole taxing power. Thereafter the sovereignty of the States and autonomy of the communities, so pointedly recognized by the framers of the Constitution and nurtured through many generations of American life, will have been changed into a subservience to Federal direction in direct proportion to their dependence upon Federal grants for local support.

Opening, Centennial Celebration,
Seattle, Washington,
November 13, 1951

More and more we work not for ourselves but for the State. In time, if permitted to continue this trend cannot fail to be destructive. For no nation may survive in freedom once its people become the servants of the State, a condition to which we are now pointed with dreadful certainty.

Labor, as always, will be the first to feel its frightful consequence.

It is quite true that some levy upon the people's earnings to pay the cost of government is unavoidable. But the costs of government, even discounting extraordinary military requirements, have risen to an accelerated, alarming and reckless rate.

Nothing is heard from those in supreme executive authority concerning the possibility of a reduction or even limitation upon these mounting costs. No suggestion deals with the restoration of some semblance of a healthy balance. No plan is advanced for easing the crushing burden already resting upon the people.

To the contrary, all that we hear are the plans by which such costs progressively may be increased. New means are constantly being devised for greater call upon the taxable potential...

Massachusetts Legislature,
Boston, Massachusetts,
July 25, 1951

The complexity brought about by dislocations in the wake of two world wars has caught our beloved country in the vortex of a confused, distressed and frightened world.

National Convention, The American Legion,
October 17, 1951

We must lead the world down this road, however long and tortuous and illusory it may now appear. Such is the role as I see it for which this great nation of ours is now cast. In this we follow the Cross. If we meet the challenge we cannot fail.

Massachusetts Legislature,
Boston, Massachusetts,
July 25, 1951

On this problem of greatest universal concern, unless we address ourselves to the fundamentals we shall get no farther than the preceding generations which have tried and failed. Convention after convention has been entered into designed to humanize war and bring it under the control of rules dictated by the highest human ideals. Yet each war becomes increasingly savage as the means for mass killing are further developed.

Massachusetts Legislature,
Boston, Massachusetts,
July 25, 1951

To this section of the country men point as the cradle of our freedom. For here was established more than three centuries ago a declaration of rights from which ultimately came the constitutional mandate guaranteeing our civil liberties. Here men arose militantly in protest against the tyranny of oppressive rule of burdensome taxation. Here men engaged in formal combat to sever the distasteful bonds of colonial rule. Here men etched the patriot's pattern which all races who harbored in their hearts a love for freedom have since sought to emulate. Here men, by their courage, vision and faith, forged a new concept of civilization.

Massachusetts Legislature,
Boston, Massachusetts,
July 25, 1951

If I could voice but one solemn warning in the lengthening shadows of life, I would point to the jeopardy to our independence by the high-handed and reckless course of foreign-dominated national policy, and urge thoughtful reflection upon General Washington's stern and realistic order at another crisis in America's past: "Let none but Americans stand guard tonight."

Michigan Legislature,
Lansing, Michigan,
May 15, 1952

The first of these principles is that every citizen is obligated to the nations defense ... No man has the inalienable right to enjoy the privileges and opportunities conferred upon him by free institutions unless he simultaneously acknowledges his duty to defend with his life and with his property the government through which he acquired these opportunities and these privileges. To deny this individual responsibility is to reject the whole theory of democratic government. This principal knows of no limitation of time or condition. It is effective in war, in peace and for as long as the nation shall endure.

The second great principle is that our national defense system must provide actual security. Indeed, an insufficient defense is almost a contradiction in terms. A dam that crumbles under the rising flood is nothing more than a desolate monument to the wasted effort and lack of vision of its builders....

The next principle to which I hold is the insistent need for current and future economy. Although there are no costs of peace comparable to those that would surely follow defeat in war, it is nevertheless incumbent upon the government to avoid unnecessary expenditure...

Circa 1936
Major General Courtney Whitney
"MacArthur: His Rendezvous with History"
Alfred A. Knopf, New York, 1956

LIFE

It (Youth)... means ... an appetite for adventure over love of ease.

Dedication, MacArthur Park,
Little Rock, Arkansas,
March 23 1952

I promise to keep on living as though I expected to live forever.

Los Angeles County Council,
The American Legion,
Los Angeles, California,
January 26, 1955

That it (education) has given you ... an appetite for adventure over love of ease;

101st Commencement, Michigan State Univ.,
Lansing, Michigan,
June 11, 1961

They (duty, honor, country) give you ... an appetite for adventure over love of ease.

U. S. Military Academy,
West Point, New York,
May 12, 1962

I have never forgotten his (Grandfather's) words, "My dear boy, nothing is sure in this life. Everything is relative."

General of the Army Douglas MacArthur
"Reminiscences"
McGraw-Hill Book Company, New York, 1964

...it is well that we remember the composite of pioneering characteristics which have gone into the building of this great American city. Here strength overcame weakness, courage dominated fear, and the responsibility of life overshadowed the certainty or death. Here, men, through an exemplification of spirituality, fashioned character as a far more meaningful and valued heritage than the material results their labors brought forth. It is that heritage of character which must be preserved by our generation so that we could do now what they did then. The American heart still harbors that same love of liberty, indomitable will and rugged determination which animated their early efforts. Yet, it would be folly compounded to ignore those internal pressures now at work to weaken that heritage of America's past.

Opening, Centennial Celebration,
Seattle, Washington,
November 13, 1951

...that it (education) has taught you to be ... humble and gentle in success.
101st Commencement, Michigan State Univ.,
Lansing, Michigan,
June 11, 1961

They (duty, honor, country) teach you to be ... humble and gentle in success.
U. S. Military Academy,
West Point, New York,
May 12, 1962

(Education has taught you) ...not to seek the path of comfort, but face the stress and spur of difficulty and challenge...
101st Commencement, Michigan State Univ.,
Lansing, Michigan,
June 11, 1961

They (duty, honor, country) teach you ... not to seek the path of comfort, but face the stress and spur of difficulty and challenge...
U. S. Military Academy,
West Point, New York,
May 12, 1962

(Education teaches you) ...to learn to stand up in the storm but feel compassion for those who fail.
101st Commencement, Michigan State Univ.,
Lansing, Michigan,
June 11, 1961

They (duty, honor, country) teach you ...to learn to stand up in the storm but to have compassion for those who fail.
U. S. Military Academy,
West Point, New York,
May 12, 1962

This is the greatest city in the world
New York, New York,
April 20, 1951

...although without command authority or responsibility, I still proudly possess that to me the greatest of all honors and distinction - I am an American
Chicago, Illinois,
April 26, 1951

It (deep spiritual urge) is an infallible reminder that our greatest hope and faith rests upon two mighty symbols - the Cross and the Flag.
Flag Day,
Houston, Texas,
June 14, 1951

All men of good conscience earnestly seek peace.

Dallas, Texas,
June 15, 1951

Let us make clear our eagerness to abolish the scourge of war from the face of the earth just a soon as others are willing to rise to so noble a stature with us.

Texas Legislature,
Austin, Texas,
June 13, 1951

If we renew our faith in the moral and ethical standards of our fathers and look for guidance from the unfailing wisdom of the people as expressed in public opinion, we will be safe.

San Antonio, Texas,
June 15, 1951

Texas, of which this great city is so vital a part, is a shining example of the power generated under conditions of human liberty.

Fort Worth, Texas,
June 16, 1951

Nowhere are men found more devoted to the concept of freedom and the preservation of the American system based upon truth and justice.

Fort Worth, Texas,
June 16, 1951

None give more hope that an America conceived in liberty will survive in liberty.

Fort Worth, Texas,
June 16, 1951

It was the adventurous spirit of America which, despite risks and hazards, carved a great nation from an almost impenetrable wilderness...

Massachusetts Legislature,
Boston, Massachusetts,
July 25, 1951

Those who lack the enterprise, vision and courage to try a new approach when none others have succeeded fail completely the simple test of leadership.

Massachusetts Legislature,
Boston, Massachusetts,
July 25, 1951

The courts must function as the champion of human justice and the police power be exercised with primary regard to individual rights.

Letter to Japanese Prime Minister,
August 20, 1951

Mr. President, I wish to express to you my thanks and deepest appreciation for the signal honor you have bestowed upon me. The field of Social Sciences which your distinguished Society represents embraces a symposium of art, culture, humanism and divinity which leads and guides both in peace and war. Its great traditions form the bulwark of modern civilization - the fruition of all man's hopes and dreams. I think you can therefore understand my pride in having my name scrolled on your tablets. You have etched for me a memory tonight I shall never forget.

National Institute of Social Science
Annual Dinner,
Waldorf-Astoria Hotel, New York, New York,
November 8, 1951

Should the pioneering spirit cease to dominate the American character, our national progress would end. For a nation's life is never static. It must advance or it will recede. Only through the indomitable will characteristic of the early American can continued development be made in the arts and sciences, in industry and agriculture, in trade and commerce, and in all those things which raise the standard of human life. The pioneering spirit finds its incentives and guiding impulse in the freedoms Americans enjoy - of opportunity, of expression and of choice in what we do - freedoms bulwarked by a constitutional charter embodying the experience and wisdom of the ages in securing the liberty, the dignity and the general welfare of each individual citizen.

Opening, Centennial Celebration,
Seattle, Washington,
November 13, 1951

The pioneering spirit finds its incentives and guiding impulse in the freedoms Americans enjoy - of expression and of choice in what we do - freedoms bulwarked by a constitutional charter embodying the experience and wisdom of the ages in securing the liberty, the dignity and the general welfare of each individual citizen.

Opening, Centennial Celebration,
Seattle, Washington,
November 13, 1951

...it is well that we remember the composite of pioneering characteristics which have gone into the building of this great American city. Here strength overcame weakness, courage dominated fear, and the responsibility of life overshadowed the certainty or death. Here, men, through an exemplification of spirituality, fashioned character as a far more meaningful and valued heritage than the material results their labors brought forth. It is that heritage of character which must be preserved by our generation so that we could do now what they did then. The American heart still harbors that same love of liberty, indomitable will and rugged determination which animated their early efforts. Yet, it would be folly compounded to ignore those internal pressures now at work to weaken that heritage of America's past.

Opening, Centennial Celebration,
Seattle, Washington,
November 13, 1951

In this historic forum I recall vividly and reverently the memory of those great architects and defenders of liberty who immortalized the Commonwealth of Massachusetts. To this section of the country men point as the cradle of our freedom.

For here was established more than three centuries ago a declaration of rights from which ultimately came the constitutional mandate guaranteeing our civil liberties. Here men arose militantly in protest against the tyranny of oppressive rule of burdensome taxation. Here men engaged in formal combat to sever the distasteful bonds of colonial rule.

Here men etched the patriot's pattern which all races who harbored in their hearts a love for freedom have since sought to emulate. Here men, by their courage, vision and faith, forged a new concept of modern civilization.

Massachusetts Legislature,
Boston, Massachusetts,
July 25, 1951

Boston is rightly famous through out the world for its courtesy and cordiality,... It has been an inspiration to visit again this birthplace of American Freedom...

City Hall,
Boston, Massachusetts,
July 26, 1951

Public criticism should be encouraged rather than suppressed as providing a powerful check against the evils of maladministration of the political power.

Letter to the Prime Minister of Japan,
August 20, 1951

Freedom of speech as an inalienable right should never be challenged unless it directly violates the laws governing libel and slander.

Letter to the Prime Minister of Japan,
August 20, 1951

Military victory had been achieved for our cause and men turned their thoughts from the task of mass killing to the higher duty of international restoration, from destroying to rebuilding, from destruction to construction.

Cleveland, Ohio,
September 6, 1951

...is American life of the future to be characterized by freedom or by servitude, strength or weakness?

Cleveland, Ohio,
September 6, 1951

I have seen in the faces of the American People that to which Mr. (Abraham) Lincoln prophetically referred. I have clearly seen that the soul of liberty is still living and vibrant in the American heart. It is neither democratic nor republican but American. It will assert itself by Constitutional process and with invincible force in the battle to save the Republic. The people will still rule.

Cleveland, Ohio,
September 6, 1951

I have an abiding faith that this nation conceived in liberty under God will mount the moral force essential to preserve its free institutions against the assaults of those bent upon their ultimate destruction.

Salvation Army,
New York City, New York,
December 12, 1951

I left Little Rock long, long years ago when life was simpler and gentler. The world has turned over many times since then and those days of old have vanished, tone and tint; they have gone glimmering through the dreams of things that were. To me their memory is a land of used to be, watered by tears and coaxed and caressed by the smiles of yesterday. It is filled with ghosts from far-off fields in khaki and olive drab, in navy blue and air corps gray. I can almost hear the faint, far whisper of their forgotten songs. Youth, strength, aspirations, struggles, triumphs, despairs, wide winds sweeping, beacons flashing across uncharted depths, faint bugles sounding reveille, far drums beating the long roll, the wail of sirens, the crash of guns, the thud of bombs, the rattle of musketry - the still white crosses!

MacArthur Park,
Little Rock, Arkansas,
March 23, 1952

Youth is not a time of life - it is a state of mind. It is not a matter of ripe cheeks, red lips and supple knees; it is a temper of the will, a quality of the imagination, a vigor of the emotions; it is a freshness of the deep springs of life.

MacArthur Park,
Little Rock, Arkansas,
March 23, 1952

Nobody grows old by merely living a number of years; people grow old by deserting their ideals. Years wrinkle the skin, but to give up enthusiasm wrinkles the soul. Worry, doubt, self-distrust, fear and despair - these are the long, long years that bow the head and turn the growing spirit back to dust.

MacArthur Park,
Little Rock, Arkansas,
March 23, 1952

Whether seventy or sixteen, there is in every being's heart the love of wonder, the sweet amazement at the stars and the star-like things and thoughts, the undaunted challenge of events, the unfailing child-like appetite for what next, and the joy and the game of life.

MacArthur Park,
Little Rock, Arkansas,
March 23, 1952

You are as young as your faith, as old as your doubt; as young as your self-confidence, as old as your fear; as young as your hope, as old as your despair.

MacArthur Park,
Little Rock, Arkansas,
March 23, 1952

In the central place of your heart there is a wireless station; so long as it receives messages of beauty, hope, cheer, courage, grandeur and power, so long you are young.

MacArthur Park,
Little Rock, Arkansas,
March 23, 1952

When the wires are all down and all the central place of your heart is covered with snows of pessimism and the ice of cynicism, then you are grown old indeed.

MacArthur Park,
Little Rock, Arkansas,
March 23, 1952

The Salvation Army - truly a defender of the faith - stirs in me memories from early childhood of ministrations to raise the fallen, to save the distressed and to strengthen the weak. Accorded but sparing public recognition, its dedication to human welfare through the years has given living meaning to the name which it bears - Salvation. It has become a mighty moral force in the life of civilized communities.

Salvation Army,
New York, New York,
December 12, 1951

While none will dispute the need for a progressive and continuous revaluation of our procedures to meet new conditions, nor the absorption of sound and enlightened ideas designed to advance the general welfare, such a callous indifference to fundamental principles long and successfully standing as the bulwark to American progress finds support in neither statesmanship nor logic. Indeed, the masses of the people in their innate wisdom have sensed and resented the tragic mishandling of their public affairs and desperately sought a reorientation toward effective security, reasonable stability and honest administration.

Michigan Legislature,
Lansing, Michigan,
May 15, 1952

We cannot relive the past. All that we can do is from its lessons of failure redesign the present in order that we may provide needed safeguards for the future.

Michigan Legislature,
Lansing, Michigan,
May 15, 1952

...that past has taught that in the crucible of freedom and opportunity, peoples of differing races and tongues may harmoniously live together and work together and prosper together.

City Hall,
Detroit, Michigan,
May 16, 1952

The working men and women of American, more perhaps than any other segment of American life, have both the responsibility of public duty and the responsibility of self-interest alike to insure that those mighty forces - spiritual, political and material - which gave them their present position of eminence in modern society and provided them with the world's beat tools and technology and working conditions are nurtured and preserved in their maximum vitality.

City Hall,
Detroit, Michigan,
May 16, 1952

...a nation is but the collective expression of the individuals which comprise it, with all of the emotions which rule the individual mind.

National Association of Manufacturers,
Waldorf-Astoria Hotel, New York, New York,
December 5, 1952

We must unite in the high purpose that the liberties etched upon the design of our life by our forefathers be unimpaired and that we maintain the moral courage and spiritual leadership to preserve inviolate that mighty bulwark of all freedom, our Christian faith.

Michigan Legislature,
Lansing, Michigan,
May 15, 1952

As always, it is the great masses of the people, not the rich or prosperous, but the farmer, the laborer, and the average office worker who suffer the most.

Opening, Centennial Celebration,
Seattle, Washington,
November 13, 1951

Some of these penalties are now obscured by the reckless extravagance of government spending which creates a false sense of security, but the day of reckoning is inevitable and understanding and fear of this injects a tragic apprehension in the American mind. Yet our leaders offer neither plan nor hope for a return to frugality and reason. Our remaining tax potential has been so depleted that, if the reckless policies of government continue unchecked, the direct confiscation of capital to meet the ensuing obligations is almost inevitable.

Opening, Centennial Celebration,
Seattle, Washington,
November 13, 1951

The will to be free either exists in the human heart or all the money in the world cannot put it there.

Thus, despite the billions we have poured abroad, I doubt that we have gained a single Communist convert to the cause of human freedom or inspired new or deeper friendships. And as, quite obviously, the people of Western Europe do not generally share with our own leaders the fear of Soviet military designs, despite these billions we seem to have made little progress in convincing them that they themselves should vigorously act to shore up their own defenses. We hear no clamor to pledge their own lives, their own fortunes and their own sacred honor in defense of their own liberties.

Mississippi Legislature,
Jackson, Mississippi,
March 22, 1952

What gullibility to think the free world would fight for freedom in Europe after refusing to do so in Asia! I am as interested in saving Western Europe as any other threatened area, where the people show the will and the determination to mount their own full defensive power.

Texas Legislature,
Austin, Texas,
June 13, 1951

The taste of freedom is a heady wine that ultimately no human being can resist.

General of the Army Douglas MacArthur
"Reminiscences"
McGraw-Hill Book Company, New York, 1964

At eighteen one wonders how little parents understand; years later, the wonder is how wise they were.

General of the Army Douglas MacArthur
"Reminiscences"
McGraw-Hill Book Company, New York, 1964

Nothing has touched me more deeply than the act of the National Father's Day committee. By profession I am a soldier and take pride in that fact, but I am prouder, infinitely prouder, to be a father. A soldier destroys in order to build; the father only builds, never destroys. The one has the potentialities of death; the other embodies creation and life. And while the hordes of death are mighty, the battalions of life are mightier still. It is my hope that my son when I am gone will remember me, not from the battle, but in the home, repeating with him our simple daily prayer, "Our Father who art in heaven...."

Statement made on selection by the National
Father's Day Committee as
"Father of The Year",
June 18, 1942

Editors note: MacArthur's reflections while traveling as aide de camp to his father on a 9 month extended tour of the far east for the War Department in 1905.

I was deeply impressed by and filled with admiration for the thrift, courtesy and friendliness of the ordinary citizen. They seemed to have discovered the dignity of labor, the fact that a man is happier and more contented when constructing than when merely idling away time.

General of the Army Douglas MacArthur
"Reminiscences"
McGraw-Hill Book Company, New York, 1964

Editors note: MacArthur's reflections while traveling as aide de camp to his father on a 9 month extended tour of the far east for the War Department in 1905.

The true historic significance and the sense of destiny that these lands of the Western Pacific and Indian Ocean now assumed became part of me. They were to color and influence all the days of my life. Here lived almost half the population of the world, with probably more than half of the raw products to sustain future generations. Here was Western civilization's last earth frontier. It was crystal clear to me that the future and, indeed the very existence of America, were irrevocably entwined with Asia and its island outposts.

General of the Army Douglas MacArthur
"Reminiscences"
McGraw-Hill Book Company, New York, 1964

... never try to regain the past, the fire will have become ashes.

General of the Army Douglas MacArthur
"Reminiscences"
McGraw-Hill Book Company, New York, 1964

Editor' note: By January 1, 1946 progress of the occupation had been so favorable MacArthur was able to issue the following statement to the people of Japan.

A New Year has come. With it, a new day dawns for Japan. No longer is the future to be settled by a few. The shackles of militarism, of feudalism, of regimentation of body and soul, have been removed. Thought control and the abuse of education are no more. All now enjoy religious freedom and the right of speech without undue restraint. Free assembly is guaranteed. The removal of this national enslavement means freedom for the people, but at the same time it imposes upon them the individual duty to think and to act on his own initiative. The masses of Japan now have the power to govern and what is done must be done by themselves.

General of the Army Douglas MacArthur
"Reminiscences"
McGraw-Hill Book Company, New York, 1964

MacArthur receives the Thanks of Congress Award, August, 1962.

PEACE

Corruption and rumors of corruption have shaken the people's trust in the integrity of those administering the civil power.

Texas Legislature,
Austin, Texas,
June 13, 1951

Our nation is young and virile and our future is still before us.

Flag Day,
Houston, Texas,
June 14, 1951

There are those who seek to subvert government from being the guardian of the people's rights, to make of it an instrument of despotic power.

Flag Day,
Houston, Texas,
June 14, 1951

...to help preserve freedom for those who have the will and determination to do all in their power to defend their own freedom; to avoid being drawn into unreasonable and unnecessary expenditures for armament to create an artificial domestic prosperity for political ends; to avoid contributing the fruits of our system of free enterprise to support socialism or communism abroad under the spurious pretense that it serves our own military security;...

National Convention, The American Legion,
Miami, Florida,
October 17, 1951

Many peoples have lost faith in our leadership, and there is a growing anxiety in the American home as disclosures reveal graft and corruption over a broad front in our public service. Those charged with its stewardship seem either apathetic, indifferent or in seeming condonation.

Opening, Centennial Celebration,
Seattle, Washington,
November 13, 1951.

At war's end the main agency for maintaining the peace became the United Nations. This organization was conceived in a common desire that the scourge of war should not again be visited upon the earth. It was dedicated to the principle that all mankind of unalienable right should live in justice and liberty and peace. It represents perhaps the noblest effort man has yet made to evolve a universal code based upon the highest of moral precepts. It became the keystone to an arch of universal hope.

Yet in practice its efforts become increasingly doubtful of ultimate success. Its organization is inherently weak, legislatively, judicially and executively. It lacks legislative strength because its members, not being elected but merely appointed, are not answerable directly to the people. It lacks judicial strength because there is no accepted international code of sufficient moral authority or purpose to mold and guide its decisions. It lacks executive strength because it controls no agencies of sufficient power to enforce its mandates.

It threatens to fail; if the innate selfishness of its members does not yield to universal needs; if the mechanics of its operations are not corrected to prevent the will of one nation from counterbalancing the collective will of the others; if it does not stop obstructionist tactics, even by expulsion if necessary, of its own unruly members; if regional military alliances must be organized within its membership to undertake collective security measures against threat from other members; if it allows itself to be reduced to a mere forum for meaningless and acrimonious debate, and a springboard for propaganda.

Unless a strong and dynamic sense of responsibility emerges within its ranks capable of rallying the forces of good throughout the world; of establishing a higher moral tone to its deliberations and activities; of correcting its existing institutional and mechanical weaknesses, the United Nations may well go the way of its predecessor League and perish as a force to guide civilization.

But the great moral and spiritual purpose which animated its formation - the abolition of war from the face of the earth - will always live and a way must be found to achieve that purpose. This way cannot be found, however, if nations are so blind as not to see their own weaknesses - so weak as not to correct them.

Cleveland, Ohio,
September 6, 1951

I am truly a mixture of the Blue and the Gray; a living symbol of that united America which largely resulted form the nobility and deep spirituality which mothers of both South and North brought to the welding of a new union between the States.

Dedication of Memorial to his Mother,
Mary Pinkney Hardy,
Norfolk, Virginia,
November 18, 1951

It is imperative that the citizen army now in the making be not corrupted by the same influences which have tended to corrupt the principle of representative government - that it be sustained on that high moral plane which befits the noble purpose it is organized to serve. This can only be if the service of the citizen soldier is held to a level of dignity and opportunity which commands his fullest measure of devotion.

Article, American Legion Magazine,
January, 1952

For modern war teaches that industry has become a main line of national defense. It has become the bulwark of human freedom.

National Association of Manufacturers,
Waldorf-Astoria Hotel, New York, New York,
December 5, 1952

This is America's Age of Triumph. The brain of man is abstracting from the Universe its fundamental secrets. There are no limits any more to production. Historic deficits are transmuted into future surpluses. So fast is progress that today's wonder is tomorrow's obsolescence. More and more! Better and better!

These things are the achievements of free men. Freedom is not merely the right to worship God in one's own way, or to speak one's mind in public places, or to move about unmanacled. It is also, most importantly, the right to create, the right to work and the right to possess the fruits of that labor. Economic freedom is the basis of all other freedoms.

National Association of Manufacturers,
Waldorf-Astoria Hotel, New York, New York,
December 5, 1952

It is imperative that we stand militantly for the most vital quality of Americanism - economic freedom.

National Association of Manufacturers,
Waldorf-Astoria Hotel, New York, New York,
December 5, 1952

Could I have but a line a century hence crediting a contribution to the advance of peace, I would gladly yield every honor which has been accorded me by war.

National Institute of Social Sciences,
Annual Dinner,
Waldorf-Astoria Hotel, New York, New York,
November 8, 1951

No one desires peace as much as the soldier, for he must pay the greatest penalty in war.

Veterans of The Rainbow (42nd) Infantry
Division of World War I,
Washington, DC,
July 14, 1935

THE PHILIPPINES

...the Philippines: the key that unlocks the door to the Pacific.

General of the Army Douglas MacArthur
"Reminiscences"
McGraw-Hill Book Company, New York, 1964

Editor's note: During the Luzon campaign in early 1941-42, MacArthur was able to delay the Japanese mass from the use of Manila and Manila Bay for nearly 6 months.

... hold long enough to force the Japanese to deploy in full force, ... slowly give way, leaving the engineers ... to dynamite bridges and construct roadblocks to bar the way. Again and again, these tactics would be repeated. Stand and fight, slip back and dynamite. It was savage and bloody, but it won time.

General of the Army Douglas MacArthur
"Reminiscences"
McGraw-Hill Book Company, New York, 1964

Of our former ward, the Philippines, we can look forward in confidence that the existing unrest will be corrected and a strong and healthy nation will grow in the longer aftermath of war's terrible destructiveness. We must be patient and understanding and never fail them, as in our hour of need they did not fail us. A Christian nation, the Philippines stand as a mighty bulwark of Christianity in the Far East, and its capacity for high moral leadership in Asia is unlimited.

U. S. Congress,
Washington, DC,
April 19, 1951

MacArthur and staff on an inspection tour at Dulag, Leyte Island, October 1944.

"I Shall Return": The well-known words "I shall return," while not made in a public address by General MacArthur, deserve mention here among some of the General's better and lesser known remarks. After leaving the Philippines March 12, 1942, MacArthur made his way to Australia where he was pressed by reporters for a statement. He issued the following statement: "The President of the United States ordered me to break through the Japanese lines and proceed from Corregidor to Australia for the purpose, as I understand it, of organizing the American offensive against Japan, a primary object of which is the relief of the Philippines. *I came through and I shall return.*" (Italics added.) MacArthur mentioned later that he made the famous remark casually enough, but the words became a psychological rallying point for the Filipinos, and for many Americans. When American forces and MacArthur returned to the Philippines in October 1944, the General's first words, spoken into a microphone, were: "People of the Philippines: I have returned. By the grace of Almighty God, our forces stand again on Philippine soil. ...." It would be difficult to exaggerate the importance of the words "I shall return" and MacArthur's prestige with the Philippine people during the years 1942-44.

From "Representative Speeches of General of the Army Douglas MacArthur" compiled by the Legislative Reference Service, Library of Congress, ordered to be printed April 29, 1964.

... I have returned. I am once again in this land that I have known so long; and amongst this people that I have loved so well. .... When your distinguished President invited me to come once again to these friendly shores, I felt as though I were at last really coming home; for it was here I lived my greatest moments and it is of here I have my greatest memories.

Arrival Manila Airport, The Philippines, July 3, 1961

...my sentimental journey has carried me through this fair land from one end almost to the other. Everywhere, I have found a growing prosperity, a growing populace, a growing destiny; everywhere, friendship and affection. ... Thank you for a wonderful reception to an old soldier and his sweetheart wife. ...

Departure Manila International Airport, The Philippines, July 12, 1961

And even now as I hail you, I must say farewell. ... For I must admit with a sense of sadness, that the deepening shadows of life cast doubt upon my ability to pledge again, "I shall return."

Independence Day Ceremonies, Manila, The Philippines, July 4, 1961

POLITICS

An army can live on short rations; it can be insufficiently clothed and housed; it can even be poorly armed and equipped; but in action it is doomed to destruction without the trained and adequate leadership of officers. An efficient and sufficient corps of officers means the difference between victory and defeat. There is nothing more expensive than an insufficient army. To build an army to be defeated by some other army is sheer folly, a complete waste of money.

Response to a Congressional proposal to cut the officer corps, 1932
General of the Army Douglas MacArthur
"Reminiscences"
McGraw-Hill Book Company, New York, 1964

Pacifism and its bedfellow, Communism, are all about us. In the theaters, newspapers and magazines, pulpits and lecture halls, schools and colleges, it hangs like a mist before the face of America, organizing the forces of unrest and undermining the morals of the working man.

Day by day this canker eats deeper into the body politic.

For the sentimentalism and emotionalism which have infested our country, we should substitute hard common sense. Pacific habits do not insure peace or immunity from national insult and aggression. Any nation that would keep its self-respect must be prepared to defend itself.

Every reasonable man knows that war is cruel and destructive, and yet very little of the fever of war will melt the veneer of our civilization. History has proved that nations once great, that neglected their national defense are dust and ashes. Where are Rome and Carthage? Where Byzantium? Where Egypt, once so great a state? Where Korea, whose death cries were unheard by the world?

Speech, University of Pittsburgh, June 8, 1932
General of the Army Douglas MacArthur
"Reminiscences"
McGraw-Hill Book Company, New York, 1964

I directed the issuance of the story (the Bataan death march) to the press, but that very day Washington forbade the release of any of the details of the prisoner-of-war atrocities. ...here was the sinister beginning of the "managed news" concept by those in power. Here was the first move against that freedom of expression so essential to liberty. It was the introduction,... of a type of censorship which can easily become a menace to a free press and a threat to the liberties of a free people.

General of the Army Douglas MacArthur
"Reminiscences"
McGraw-Hill Book Company, New York, 1964

The pioneering spirit finds its incentives and guiding impulse in the freedoms Americans enjoy - of opportunity, of expression and of choice in what we do - freedoms bulwarked by a constitutional charter embodying the experience and wisdom of the ages in securing the liberty, the dignity and the general welfare of each individual citizen.

Opening, Centennial Celebration,
Seattle, Washington,
November 13, 1951.

To the early pioneer the Pacific coast marked the end of his courageous westerly advance - to us it should mark but the beginning. To him it delimited our western frontier - to us that frontier has been moved beyond the Pacific horizon.

Opening, Centennial Celebration,
Seattle, Washington,
November 13, 1951.

The issues which today confront the nation are clearly defined and so fundamental as to directly involve the very survival of the Republic.

Cleveland, Ohio,
September 6, 1951

Are we going to maintain our present course toward State socialism with communism just beyond or reverse the present trend and regain our hold upon our heritage of liberty and freedom?

Cleveland, Ohio,
September 6, 1951

Our political stature built upon wise and self-effacing   statesmanship and sound domestic policy, has been sadly impaired by a succession of diplomatic blunders abroad and reckless spendthrift aims at home.

Opening, Centennial Celebration,
Seattle, Washington,
November 13, 1951

Many peoples have lost faith in our leadership, and there is a growing anxiety in the American home as disclosures reveal graft and corruption over a broad front in our public service. Those charged with its stewardship seem either apathetic, indifferent or in seeming condonation.

Opening, Centennial Celebration,
Seattle, Washington,
November 13, 1951

Freedom of speech and expression are no longer untrammeled. Slanted propaganda and abusive language are used to suppress criticism of the public administration and discourage dissemination of the truth

Opening, Centennial Celebration,
Seattle, Washington,
November 13, 1951

Expenditure upon expenditure, extravagance upon extravagance have so burdened our people with taxation and fed the forces of inflation that our traditionally high standard of life has become largely fictitious and illusory. Apart from the direct income tax impounded at source, every necessity of life gives constant warning of the diminishing value of both national currency and private income. As always, it is the great masses of the people, not the rich or the prosperous, but the farmer, the laborer and the average office worker who suffer the most.

Opening, Centennial Celebration,
Seattle, Washington,
November 13, 1951

It must be all or nothing; the traditional American way of life or a totalitarian concept imported from abroad. All other issues are but secondary to this one which strikes at the very roots of our personal liberties and representative form of government.

Opening, Centennial Celebration,
Seattle, Washington,
November 13, 1951

...Socialism, once a reality, destroys that moral fiber which is the creation of freedom.

Opening, Centennial Celebration,
Seattle, Washington,
November 13, 1951

This carnival (seeking personal political power through preferential treatment) of special privilege cannot fail to undermine our heritage of character.

Opening, Centennial Celebration,
Seattle, Washington,
November 13, 1951

The great bulwark of the Republic, individual and collective self-reliance, is under constant threat through a carefully designed and progressive paternalism which renders both community and individual increasingly dependent upon the support of the Federal Government. In all areas of private welfare, the Socialist planners seek to inject the Federal hand to produce a progressive weakening of the structure of individual character. The area of possible resistance to this creeping sabotage of freedom is being constantly narrowed as the Federal Government arrogates to itself more and more of the remaining tax potential.

Opening, Centennial Celebration,
Seattle, Washington,
November 13, 1951

There is an almost insatiate demand for money to finance policies seemingly designed but to spend and spend and spend.

Opening, Centennial Celebration,
Seattle, Washington,
November 13, 1951

It has been truly said, "the power to tax is the power to destroy."

It is, perhaps, the most sinister of all political powers...

As such, it has been possibly the greatest single cause of political revolt throughout the history of the human race.

Indeed, the fundamental issue which precipitated our American Revolution was the arbitrary and oppressive tax levy by the British Crown.

Opening, Centennial Celebration,
Seattle, Washington,
November 13, 1951

The Japanese people, since the war (WW II), have undergone the greatest reformation recorded in modern history.

U. S. Congress,
Washington, DC,
April 19, 1951

I have no political aspirations whatsoever.

City Hall,
San Francisco, California,
April 18, 1951

It is for future events to ascertain whether they (the American people) still retain the ultimate authority over government as intended by the constitution or whether such authority has been lost in the drift from the patterns ordained by the architects of our political institutions.

Chicago, Illinois,
April 26, 1951

...enemy bullets have no respect for political affiliation and strike down the son of a Democrat just as surely as the son of a Republican.

Chicago, Illinois,
July 26, 1951

They (our soldiers) died that mortal ideals might not perish.

Milwaukee, Wisconsin,
April 27, 1951

It (war monument) will constantly remind of those sacred and immutable concepts - liberty, justice and truth...

Milwaukee, Wisconsin,
April 27, 1951

His (Soviet) intrigue has found its success... in the moral weakness of the free world.

Texas Legislature,
Austin, Texas,
June 13, 1951

There are those who call piously for unity even while doing so much to prevent unity.

Texas Legislature,
Austin, Texas, June 13, 1951

...I am concerned for the security of our great Nation, not so much because of any potential threat from without, but because of the insidious forces working from within which, opposed all the great traditions, have gravely weakened the structure and tone of our American way of life.

Milwaukee, Wisconsin,
April 27, 1951

The world should have common sense enough, when it surveys the last two wars, to understand that war has become incompatible with the survival of modern civilization.

Milwaukee, Wisconsin,
April 27, 1951

...no administration in a republic can long defy the public opinion when adequately and vigorously expressed.

Dallas, Texas,
June 15, 1951

There are those who plan to alter the constitutional checks and balances established to preserve the integrity of our coordinate branches.

Flag Day,
Houston, Texas,
June 14, 1951

There are those who seek to convert us to a form of socialistic endeavor leading to the path of Communist slavery.

Flag Day,
Houston, Texas,
June 14, 1951

The Alamo! On this hallowed soil at a crucial moment in history a small band of Texans stood and died rather than yield the precious concept of liberty.

San Antonio, Texas,
June 15, 1951

Suppress the truth, curtail free expression and you destroy the basis of all the freedoms.

San Antonio, Texas,
June 15, 1951

All must rally to the demand that administration of the civil power be on a level of morality which will command the public confidence and faith.

Fort Worth, Texas,
June 16, 1951

National policy (should) be determined with primary regard to the ultimate well being of our own people.

Fort Worth, Texas,
June 16, 1951

The drift upward in the cost of bureaucracy and the expenditure of public funds in complete disregard of the tax burden has accelerated so alarmingly that the people are rapidly becoming the servants of the state.

Fort Worth,
Texas, June 16, 1951

The drift toward Socialism through indirect internal pressures faces us with the inevitable collapse of individual incentive and full personal energy.

Fort Worth, Texas,
June 16, 1951

Petty corruption in the public administration is a disease unfortunately common to all nations...

Massachusetts Legislature,
Boston, Massachusetts,
July 25, 1951

Men of significant stature in national affairs appear to cower before the threat of reprisal if the truth be expressed in criticism of those in higher public authority.

Massachusetts Legislature,
Boston, Massachusetts,
July 25, 1951

...war is outmoded as an instrument of political policy.

Massachusetts Legislature,
Boston, Massachusetts,
July 25, 1951

...it (War) provides no solution for international problems.

Massachusetts Legislature,
Boston, Massachusetts,
July 25, 1951

While we must be prepared to meet the trial of war if war comes, we should gear our foreign and domestic policies toward the ultimate goal - the abolition of war from the face of the earth.

Massachusetts Legislature,
Boston, Massachusetts,
July 25, 1951

Therein lies our best hope in the battle to save America - the full weight of an aroused, informed and militant public opinion.

Massachusetts Legislature,
Boston, Massachusetts,
July 25, 1951

Restraint and frugality in the use of the public purse produces economic stability, encourages individual thrift and minimizes the burden of tax action.

Letter to Japanese Prime Minister,
August 20, 1951

Avoidance of the excessive centralization of the political power safeguards against the danger of totalitarian rule with the suppression of personal liberty, advances the concept of local autonomy and develops an acute consciousness in the individual citizen of his political responsibility. Undue paternalism in government tends to sap the creative potential and impair initiative and energy in those who thereby come to regard governmental subsidy as an inalienable right.

Letter to Japanese Prime Minister,
August 20, 1951

Of all issues which today confront our people, possibly none is of more immediate concern to the Legion than is the direction of our military policy.

National Convention, The American Legion,
Miami, Florida,
October 17, 1951

Our leaders must throw off the complacent belief that the only threat to our survival is from without.

National Convention, The American Legion,
Miami, Florida,
October 17, 1951

All freedoms lost since war's end (WW II) have been the result of internal pressures rather than external assault.

National Convention, The American Legion,
Miami, Florida,
October 17, 1951

Could there be anything more discouraging and shocking to our soldiers on the line than the deprecating reference to their fierce and savage struggle as a "police action"?

Could anything be more agonizing to the mothers of the dead than the belittling reference to it by the Joint Chiefs of Staff as the "Korean Skirmish?"

National Convention, The American Legion,
Miami, Florida,
October 17, 1951

Two great questions about Korea still remain unanswered. First why did they start the war if they did not intend to win it? And second, what do they intend to do now? ... Hardened old soldier though I am - my very soul revolts at the unnecessary slaughter of the flower of our youth.

National Convention, The American Legion,
Miami, Florida,
October 17, 1951

(We must) curb the growing tendency of political and military leaders to publicize for political advantage classified data concerning scientific developments incident to our military effort and thus to yield the all important element of surprise.

National Convention, The American Legion,
Miami, Florida,
October 17, 1951

The threat to freedom in peace is no less sinister than in war.

National Convention, The American Legion,
Miami, Florida,
October 17, 1951

In short, is American life of the future to be characterized by freedom or by servitude, strength or weakness. The answer must be clear and unequivocal if we are to avoid the pitfalls toward which we are heading with such certainty. In many respects it is not to be found in any dogma of political philosophy but in those immutable precepts which underlie the Ten Commandments.

Cleveland, Ohio,
September 6, 1951

Avoid distributing our wealth for the purpose of buying the loyalty of others, or of sharing with others the wealth and security which we hold in sacred trust for our progeny.

National Convention, The American Legion,
Miami, Florida,
October 17, 1951

Freedom of speech and expression are no longer untrammeled. Slanted propaganda and abusive language are used to suppress criticism of the public administration and discourage dissemination of the truth.

Opening, Centennial Celebration,
Seattle, Washington,
November 13, 1951

Expenditure upon expenditure, extravagance upon extravagance have so burdened our people with taxation and fed the forces of inflation that our traditionally high standard of life has become largely fictitious and illusory. Apart from the direct income tax impounded at source, every necessity of life gives constant warning of the diminishing value of both national currency and private income. As always, it is the great masses of the people, not the rich or the prosperous, but the farmer, the laborer and the average office worker who suffer the most.

Opening, Centennial Celebration,
Seattle, Washington,
November 13, 1951

It must be all or nothing; the traditional American way of life or a totalitarian concept imported from abroad. All other issues are but secondary to this one which strikes at the very roots of our personal liberties and representative form of government.

Opening, Centennial Celebration,
Seattle, Washington,
November 13, 1951

...Socialism, once a reality, destroys that moral fiber which is the creation of freedom.

Opening, Centennial Celebration,
Seattle, Washington,
November 13, 1951

It (Socialism) discourages development of those moral forces which would preserve inviolate our representative form of government, answerable to the free will of the electorate.

Opening, Centennial Celebration,
Seattle, Washington,
November 13, 1951

The great bulwark of the Republic, individual and collective self-reliance, is under constant threat through a carefully designed and progressive paternalism which renders both community and individual increasingly dependent upon the support of the Federal Government. In all areas of private welfare, the Socialist planners seek to inject the Federal hand to produce a progressive weakening of the structure of individual character. The area of possible resistance to this creeping sabotage of freedom is being constantly narrowed as the Federal Government arrogates to itself more and more of the remaining tax potential.

Opening, Centennial Celebration,
Seattle, Washington,
November 13, 1951

There is an almost insatiate demand for money to finance policies seemingly designed but to spend and spend and spend.

Opening, Centennial Celebration,
Seattle, Washington,
November 13, 1951

It has been truly said, "the power to tax is the power to destroy."

Opening, Centennial Celebration,
Seattle, Washington,
November 13, 1951

It (power to tax) is, perhaps, the most sinister of all political powers.

Opening, Centennial Celebration,
Seattle, Washington,
November 13, 1951

As such, it (power to tax) has been possibly the greatest single cause of political revolt throughout the history of the human race.

Opening, Centennial Celebration,
Seattle, Washington,
November 13, 1951

Indeed, the fundamental issue which precipitated our American Revolution was the arbitrary and oppressive tax levy by the British Crown.

Opening, Centennial Celebration,
Seattle, Washington,
November 13, 1951

I was just asked if I intended to enter politics - my reply was "no" - I have no political aspirations whatsoever. I do not intend to run for any political office and I hope that my name will never be used in a political way. The only politics I have is contained in a simple phrase - known well by all of you - "God Bless America."

City Hall,
San Francisco, California,
April 18, 1951

What is our policy in Korea? Some will tell you that the pacification and unification of all Korea is the objective - an objective which indeed still stands as the formal mandate of the United Nations. Others tend to overlook such a formally stated policy and will tell you that our objective is achieved upon clearing South Korea of invading forces. Still others ignore both explanations and frankly say that our objective now is to continue to engage the enemy forces in Korea in a prolonged and indecisive campaign of attrition notwithstanding the constantly increasing cost in American blood. Who will tell you in the traditionally ringing tones of the American patriot that our objective is victory over the nation and men who, without provocation or justification, have warred against us and that our forces will be furnished all the sinews and other means essential to achieve that victory with a minimum of cost in human life? The tragedy is that since the advent of the war with Red China there has been no definition of the political policy which would provide a solution for the new problems thereby created. This has resulted in a policy vacuum heretofore unknown to war.

Chicago, Illinois,
April 26, 1951

It is in this situation (lack of political policy regarding Korea) of complete unrealism that, while meticulously implementing the directives given me, I have strongly urged the need for a positive policy attuned to the military realities and designed to stop, through strength, this slaughter of America's sons.

Chicago, Illinois,
April 26, 1951

I have endeavored since my return home to keep the issue (Korea) on a higher level than partisan politics.

Chicago, Illinois,
April 26, 1951

...enemy bullets have no respect for political affiliation and strike down the son of a Democrat just as surely as the son of a Republican.

Chicago, Illinois,
April 26, 1951

I shall work with you in the discharge of our common responsibilities of citizenship to the end that American policy be based upon the thoughts and needs and aspirations of the American people, unyielding to undue political pressures from abroad. I shall stand with you for an America rededicated to those sacred and immutable ideals and concepts which guided our forefathers when drawing the design of American freedom. For although without command authority or responsibility, I still proudly possess that to me the greatest of all honors and distinctions - I am an American!

Chicago, Illinois,
April 26, 1951

If, however, we be so weak in fact that we must cower before the verbal banishments of others, the responsibility for such weakness should be a matter of the gravest public concern. Who, we should ask, is responsible for the reduction of our military strength from the greatest on earth at war's end to that they now estimate is inadequate even to support our moral commitments?

Texas Legislature,
Austin, Texas,
June 13, 1951

I am as intensely interested in saving Western Europe as any other threatened area, where the people show the will and the determination to mount their own full defensive power, but I believe the issue to be world wide and not confined to any special privileged area.

Texas Legislature,
Austin, Texas,
June 13, 1951

The defenders of the existing policy vacuum are the same who suddenly and without slightest preparation or seeming consideration of the military and political potentialities, threw us into the conflict. These are the very men who, in the face of mounting peril, deliberately demobilized us at the peak of our military strength, and then at the lowest point of our disarmament with no slightest preparation or word of warning, plunged us into a war which they now seem afraid to win.

Texas Legislature,
Austin, Texas,
June 13, 1951

There are those who call piously for unity even while doing so much to prevent unity. Unity is indeed what all Americans earnestly desire - but unity of the American brand based upon considered judgment on what best serves the national interest and reflecting full freedom of thought and expression - not unity obtained through the whip-lash of arbitrary power, with its devices for sowing fear and suppressing knowledge. Unity instead must come from the common effort to crystalize ideas and search for and publish the truth.

Texas Legislature,
Austin, Texas,
June 13, 1951

I am concerned over the position publicly taken by some of our leaders, for the first time in American history, that we are not prepared if necessary to defend ourselves. If we become actuated by fear - if we endeavor to obtain converts to policies resting upon fear through the spread of fear by propagandizing our own destruction, so long will we have that fear to contend with and to threaten us.

This great nation of ours was never more powerful - never more prepared to extend a dynamic and courageous leadership to guide the world through the morass of artificially created timidity, complexity and indecision - it never had less reason for fear. It was never more able to meet the exacting tests of leadership in peace or in war, spiritually, physically or materially. As it is yet unconquered, so is it unconquerable. Its history still lies ahead. Our finest hours are yet to come.

Texas Legislature,
Austin, Texas,
June 13, 1951

It is not from threat of external attack that we have reason for fear. It is from those insidious forces working from within. It is they that create the basis for fear by spreading false propaganda designed to destroy those moral precepts to which we have clung for direction since the immutable declaration of our independence became the great charter of our liberty.

Flag Day,
Houston, Texas,
June 14, 1951

There are those who seek to make all men servants of the State.

Flag Day,
Houston, Texas,
June 14, 1951

...so inordinate has been the application of the executive power that members of the armed services have been subjected to the most arbitrary and ruthless treatment for daring to speak the truth in accordance with conviction and conscience.

Massachusetts Legislature,
Boston, Massachusetts,
July 25, 1951

In Korea, despite the magnificent performance of our fighting forces, the result has been indecisive. The high moral purpose which so animated and inspired the world a year ago yielded to the timidity and fear of our leaders as after defeating our original enemy a new one entered the field which they dared not fight to a decision. Appeasement thereafter became the policy of war on the battlefield.

In the actual fighting with this new enemy we did not lose but neither did we win. Yet, it can be accepted as a basic principle proven and reproven since the beginning of time that a great nation which enters upon war and fails to see it through to victory must accept the full moral consequences of defeat.

Massachusetts Legislature,
Boston, Massachusetts,
July 25, 1951

While we must be prepared to meet the trial of war if war comes, we should gear our foreign and domestic policies toward the ultimate goal - the abolition of war from the face of the earth.

Massachusetts Legislature,
Boston, Massachusetts,
July 25, 1951

Those who lack the enterprise, vision and courage to try a new approach when none others have succeeded fail completely the most simple test of leadership.

Massachusetts Legislature,
Boston, Massachusetts,
July 25, 1951

Our forces were rapidly and completely demobilized and the great stores of war materiel which had been accumulated were disposed of with irresponsible waste and abandon.

Cleveland, Ohio,
September 6, 1951

Our great military victory has been offset, largely because of military unpreparedness, by the political successes of the Kremlin. Our diplomatic blunders increased as our senseless disarmament became a reality.

And now the disastrous cycle is completed as those same leaders who lost to the world the one great chance it has had for enduring universal peace, frantically endeavor, by arousing a frenzy of fear throughout the land, to gear anew our energies and resources, to rebuild our dissipated strength and to face again a future of total war.

Cleveland, Ohio,
September 6, 1951

The issues which today confront the nation are clearly defined and so fundamental as to directly involve the very survival of the Republic.

Cleveland, Ohio,
September 6, 1951

Are we going to continue to yield personal liberties and community autonomy to the steady and inexplorable centralization of all political power or restore the Republic to constitutional direction, regain our personal liberties and reassume the individual State's primary responsibility and authority in the conduct of local affairs?

Cleveland, Ohio,
September 6, 1951

...to curb the growing tendency of political and military leaders to publicize for political advantage classified data concerning scientific developments incident to our military effort, and thus to yield the all important element of surprise;...

National Convention, The American Legion,
Miami, Florida,
October 17, 1951

...give primary concern to our own security and the well being of our own people; ...avoid distributing our wealth for the purpose of buying the loyalty of others, or of sharing with others the wealth and security which we hold in sacred trust for our progeny;...

National Convention, The American Legion,
Miami, Florida,
October 17, 1951

I do not associate myself with those who believe that World War Three is imminent or inevitable, nor do I associate myself with those who hysterically talk of American cities being laid waste. I believe that this nation has such potential strength, both spiritual and material, that no power or combination of powers would dare directly to attack it.

National Convention, The American Legion,
Miami, Florida,
October 17, 1951

Such possibilities seem however beyond the comprehension of some high in our governmental circles who still feel that the Pacific coast marks the practical terminus of our advance and the westerly boundary of our immediate national interest - that any opportunity for the expansion of our foreign trade should be mainly in the area of Europe and the Middle East. Nothing could more surely put a brake upon our growth as a strong and prosperous nation. Intentionally or not, it would yield to industrialized Europe the undisputed dominion over the trade and commerce of the Far East. More than this, it would in time surrender to European nations the moral, if not political, leadership of the Eastern Hemisphere. Nothing could more clearly attest a marked recession from that far-sighted vision which animated the pioneer of one hundred years ago.

Opening, Centennial Celebration,
Seattle, Washington,
November 13, 1951

...Socialism, once a reality, destroys that moral fiber which is the creation of freedom. It breeds every device which produces totalitarian rule. It is true that our Constitution established checks and balances designed to safeguard against such dangers, but such safeguard is ignored by those who seek to entrench personal political power through preferential treatment for some at the general expense of all. This carnival of special privilege cannot fail to undermine our heritage of character. It discourages development of those moral forces which would preserve inviolate our representative form of government, answerable to the free will of the electorate.

Opening, Centennial Celebration,
Seattle, Washington,
November 13, 1951

In all areas of private welfare, the Socialist planners seek to inject the Federal hand to produce a progressive weakening of the structure of individual character.

The area of possible resistance to this creeping sabotage of freedom is being constantly narrowed as the Federal Government arrogates to itself more and more of the remaining tax potential. There is an almost insatiate demand for money to finance policies seemingly designed but to spend and spend and spend.

Opening, Centennial Celebration,
Seattle, Washington,
November 13, 1951

It has been truly said, "the power to tax is the power to destroy." It is, perhaps, the most sinister of all political powers. Administered despotically, it can and oft' times has become an instrument of tyranny and oppression. As such, it has been possibly the greatest single cause of political revolt throughout the history of the human race. Indeed, the fundamental issue which precipitated our American Revolution was the arbitrary and oppressive tax levy by the British Crown.

Opening, Centennial Celebration,
Seattle, Washington,
November 13, 1951

The greatest hazard under which we now labor is the fear that the policy and propaganda of our present leadership may be setting the stage for a third world war. We are following the same path - the same historical record - the same political concept and leadership - which projected us into World War I, World War II, and the war in Korea.

Opening, Centennial Celebration,
Seattle, Washington,
November 13, 1951

...we cannot be satisfied with a leadership which declaims a devotion to peace with constant platitudinous statements and phrases while taking steps which inexorably tend to lead toward war.

Opening, Centennial Celebration,
Seattle, Washington,
November 13, 1951

We resent the docile acceptance of abusive pressure against us without the application of adequate counter pressure available to us.

Opening, Centennial Celebration,
Seattle, Washington,
November 13, 1951

We condemn the effort to avoid possible public criticism by cloaking administrative functions behind a screen of secrecy under the doubtful pretext that the national security is directly involved.

Opening, Centennial Celebration,
Seattle, Washington,
November 13, 1951

Moral decay and political irresponsibility have penetrated the roots of our cherished institutions.

Salvation Army,
New York , New York,
December 12, 1951

We still enter wars tragically unprepared, and theretofore have found ourselves entirely lacking in that degree of military strength essential to preserve the peace. At war's end we still demobilize in haste and divest ourselves of accumulated war materiel with reckless abandon. We still lack a realistic appraisal of future potentialities, and saddle our people with wholly uncalled for burdens to cover past errors by replacing anew the power we have squandered and dissipated in the afterglow of victory. There could be no more serious indictment of our political and military leadership than this failure to profit from the clear lessons of experience. It is a failure which following World War II, still vivid in the American mind, lost us the fruits of victory and brought to us a sense of insecurity hardly surpassed in midst of war itself.

Article, American Legion Magazine,
January, 1952

It is essential that the traditional role of the Army in these distressing times be carefully preserved - that it be not used as an instrument of tyranny or oppression - a form of pretorian guard - by those seeking to strengthen and entrench personal political power - but that it be used instead as a force of free men dedicated to its sworn purpose of defending the "Constitution of the United States against all enemies, foreign and domestic."

Article, American Legion Magazine,
January, 1952

Politics were but the means toward the selection of competent leaders.

Mississippi Legislature,
Jackson, Mississippi,
March 22, 1952

History records that human liberty has oft' times been destroyed by the sword, but never before by a disingenuous application of constitutional powers expressly designed to ensure its preservation.

Mississippi Legislature,
Jackson, Mississippi,
March 22, 1952

American now stands at a crossroads. Down one lies a return to those immutable principles and ideals upon which rested our country's past grandeur. Down the other lies the arbitrary rule of men leading to the ultimate loss of constitutional liberty.

Mississippi Legislature,
Jackson, Mississippi,
March 22, 1952

Other issues which deeply stir the conscience of the American people are many and varied, but all stem from irresponsibility in leadership. Domestic policy is largely dictated by the political expediencies of the moment. Foreign policy is as shifting as the sands before the winds and tides. Spendthriftness and waste have lost us our heritage of stability, weakness and vacillation, the moral leadership of the world.

Mississippi Legislature,
Jackson, Mississippi,
March 22, 1952

The domestic scene has witnessed the greatest orgy of spending in history - a fantastic phenomenon which defies all reason - which has indiced a tax burden upon the people, largely upon the lower and middle income groups, which has already destroyed the opportunity to build for future security and is rapidly destroying the will to work. Yet, our leaders show not the slightest concern for the stark tragedy which will descend upon the nation once the exhaustion of our resources brings this extravaganza of spending to an abrupt end. Then, will our people face the reality that their energies and those of their children and children's children have been mortgaged for generations to come.

Mississippi Legislature,
Jackson, Mississippi,
March 22, 1952

Indeed, the relationship which once existed between government and people when the open criticism of the conduct of public affairs was accepted as a safe-guard against inefficient, irresponsible or arbitrary administration is now all but lost. The people are told in effect that the administration of their government is none of their affair. They are but to listen and to obey. The inner circles of government partake more and more of the nature of a pampered, exclusive club. Dangerous experiments with the public interest, creeping corruption in fiscal honesty and reckless gambling with the public security have led us inexorably down the orad toward moral decadence and political disintegration.

Mississippi Legislature,
Jackson, Mississippi,
March 22, 1952

Our failure has been of the spirit, not of the arms - a bankruptcy of leadership in our American tradition.

Mississippi Legislature,
Jackson, Mississippi,
March 22, 1952

Now it (America) faces possibly its greatest modern test if our heritage of faith is to be preserved and our liberties survive. In this time of faltering leader-ship, it is the people themselves who must meet this challenge and rechart the nation's course. For Lincoln's admonition has been proved and reproved through successive generations - that the people are wiser than their leaders.

Michigan Legislature,
Lansing, Michigan,
May 15, 1952

There is no politics in me, nor none intended in what I say. I plead nothing but Americanism.

Michigan Legislature,
Lansing, Michigan,
May 15, 1952

We have strayed far indeed from the course of constitutional liberty if it be seriously contended that patriotism has become a partisan issue in contemporary American life. Yet, only recently, the indifference, if not the contempt, held by some in high authority for the Constitution and the wisdom of its architects, and the high principles and moral codes which in past have guided and insured our national progress, was graphically emphasized by reference to the advocacy of their restoration to American life as an antiquated and outmoded point of view - a "dinosaur" point of view was the actual sarcasm employed.

Michigan Legislature,
Lansing, Michigan,
May 15, 1952

Nothing threatens us more acutely than our financial irresponsibility and reckless spendthrift policies which jeopardize all thrift and frugality. Our leaders seek to justify the high, unreasonable and burdensome costs of government on the grounds of its complexity under modern conditions. This is fallacious reasoning.

> *Michigan Legislature,*
> *Lansing, Michigan,*
> *May 15, 1952*

A return to a diffusion of the political power so wisely ordained by the constitution, leaving to the community the management of its local affairs, and to the citizen the management of his personal life, would largely relieve this complexity.

> *Michigan Legislature,*
> *Lansing, Michigan,*
> *May 15, 1952*

If the incentive to carry forward the dynamic progress this nation has registered in past is to continue and insure accelerating progress in future, the entire burden of taxation must be further materially reduced. Indeed, a reasonable limit must be placed upon the very exercise of the power to tax, easily the most abused and, as history has shown, the most dangerous of all sovereign powers.

> *Michigan Legislature,*
> *Lansing, Michigan,*
> *May 15, 1952*

We must avoid confiscating incomes and draining resources to the point that the private ownership of property will practically disappear from our economic system. We have so burdened our people with taxation that they are no longer able to build for old age and family security, and are rapidly losing the energizing incentive to work.

> *Michigan Legislature,*
> *Lansing, Michigan,*
> *May 15, 1952*

Talk of imminent threat to our national security through the application of external force is pure nonsense. Our threat is from the insidious forces working from within...

> *Michigan Legislature,*
> *Lansing, Michigan,*
> *May 15, 1952*

Through the increasing centralization of the political authority in the Federal Government and the long tenure of one group in public office, the disease of personal power has become deeply rooted. The effort to perpetuate that power through the patronage of money against which Thomas Jefferson so clearly warned has made undeniable progress in corrupting the body politic.

> *Michigan Legislature,*
> *Lansing, Michigan,*
> *May 15, 1952*

Indeed, so open and menacing have the efforts become in our country to stifle opposition, suppress the issues and enforce arbitrary and bi-partisan acceptance of entrenched public policy that we now find some of the leaders of one party openly endorsing their own selection as the nominee of the opposition party.

Michigan Legislature,
Lansing, Michigan,
May 15, 1952

...we have but recently witnessed the stark reality of tragedy and distress brought to thousands of American homes over the area of eight states by the inundation of flood waters from the Missouri and Mississippi Rivers. Such tragedy could and should have been avoided.

Michigan Legislature,
Lansing, Michigan,
May 15, 1952

I recall over forty years ago working as an engineer officer on plans for the control of just such flood conditions. Such plans have long been perfected and engineers, both military and civilian, time and time gain have appealed for the funds needed for the control measures indicated. But such funds were never forthcoming for so essential a protection of our own people, even though we remitted funds in far greater amounts to the peoples of Western Europe for purposes which included the consummation of similar protective projects.

Michigan Legislature,
Lansing, Michigan,
May 15, 1952

...every dollar we send abroad must be extracted from the sweat and toil, sacrifice and venture, of all of the American people, not only of this generation, but of the generations yet to follow. This is but one of the many cases wherein policy has furthered the interests of others at the expense of our own.

Michigan Legislature,
Lansing, Michigan,
May 15, 1952

...the tendency may grow under the influence of political pressures to reverse the process and attempt the exploitation of industry by labor. Nothing could more thoroughly wreck labor's gains of the past century. For the exploitation of industry would in time destroy the very foundations upon which those gains have rested.

City Hall,
Detroit, Michigan,
May 16, 1952

They (the working men and women of America) must resist experimentation by Government designed to replace our traditional freedom of competitive opportunity with collectivist theories and practices which have never successfully met the practical test of creating higher standards of human life.

City Hall,
Detroit, Michigan,
May 16, 1952

They (the working men and women of America) must resist the spendthrift policies of Government which may bring us to the brink of economic chaos and are forcing upon us an irresponsible economy apparently to avoid the political impact of a return to the long-range protection of frugality and reason.

City Hall,
Detroit, Michigan,
May 16, 1952

They (the working men and women of America) must resist being betrayed into political indebtedness through the bestowal of special privilege unrelated to the general welfare by those exercising the political power of Government.

City Hall,
Detroit, Michigan,
May 16, 1952

They (the working men and women of America) must insure that Government be reduced to the simplest and most economical form consistent with reasonable efficiency. This can be dome through a diffusion of the political power as wisely ordained by the constitution and the lifting of arbitrary and unreasonable controls now imposed upon community and individual citizen.

City Hall,
Detroit, Michigan,
May 16, 1952

They (the working men and women of America) must insure that Government be limited in its exercise of the taxing power to securing only the revenue needed to defray the legitimate expense of a frugal public administration and be deprived of the authority to advance the Communist concept of sharing the wealth and threatening the principal of private ownership of property through confiscatory levies upon capital, income and estates.

City Hall,
Detroit, Michigan,
May 16, 1952

They (the working men and women of America) must insure that government be required to orient basic policy toward the preservation and strengthening of our economic system based upon free, private, competitive enterprise. Government must avoid any action directed at undermining or reducing the incentive to maximize initiative and energy or to restrict the opportunities for our youth to build toward future security and family protection.

City Hall,
Detroit, Michigan,
May 16, 1952

....every move they make to circumvent the spirit of the Constitution, every move they make to centralize political power, every move they make to curtail and suppress individual liberty is reaction in its most extreme form.

For the framers of the Constitution were the most liberal thinkers of all the ages and the Charter they produced out of the liberal revolution of their time has never been and is not now surpassed in liberal thought.

Keynote Address,
Republic National Convention,
Chicago, Illinois,
July 7, 1952

They who trample upon constitutional liberty by the undue centralization and imposition of political power are turning back the pages of history and gradually reinstituting those very excesses and abuses for which the British Crown was indicted in 1776 by our Declaration of Independence. They are the dangerous reactionaries in contemporary American politics.

Keynote Address,
Republic National Convention,
Chicago, Illinois,
July 7, 1952

They have trifled with that great American institution - free, private, competitive enterprise, keystone to the arch of our economic strength as a nation and prosperity as a people.

Keynote Address,
Republic National Convention,
Chicago, Illinois,
July 7, 1952

In this march away from our traditional American standards, few of our former liberties have been left unimpaired. Rights and powers specifically reserved to state, community and individual by constitutional mandate have been ruthlessly suppressed by a creeping Federal authority. Reckless abuse indeed has been made of that most dangerous of all sovereign powers - the power to tax.

Keynote Address,
Republic National Convention,
Chicago, Illinois,
July 7, 1952

Was there ever greater hypocrisy than that which flows from those who castigate private capitalism as an evil to be renounced by human society while avidly seeking to ensnare its benefits - those who regard American dollars as the panacea for all economic ills while denouncing and condemning the source of such wealth - those who seek American goods while scoffing at and deriding the very institutions by which those goods are produced?

National Association of Manufacturers,
Waldorf-Astoria Hotel, New York, New York,
December 5, 1952

Another and yet more serious form of assault upon the capitalistic system has been the increasingly oppressive government levies upon both capital and profit. The principle underlying such levies has not been to equalize the burden of meeting the legitimate costs of government by a just and uniform assessment, but has followed instead a conspiratal design originally evolved by Karl Marx to first weaken and then destroy the capitalistic system. Thus, many of our tax laws amount in practical effect to a series of graduated penalties upon the efficiency and the thrift which produces profit and accumulates capital -penalties which strike at the very roots of the incentive to labor, to create and to cheerfully accept the risks and hazards of enterprise in the traditional American pioneering spirit.

National Association of Manufacturers,
Waldorf-Astoria Hotel, New York, New York,
December 5, 1952

We must recognize that the very survival of freedom, as the concept best ensuring the continuity of human progress, is now largely dependent upon a strong and vibrant American industrial economy, soundly rooted in a free and competitive system of private capitalism.

National Association of Manufacturers,
Waldorf-Astoria Hotel, New York, New York,
December 5, 1952

Our prestige abroad has reached a tragically low ebb and our leadership is little wanted.

Texas Legislature,
Austin, Texas,
June 13, 1951

All men of good conscience earnestly seek peace.

Dallas, Texas,
June 15, 1951

There are those who seek to subvert government from being the guardian of the people's rights, to make of it an instrument of despotic power.

Flag Day,
Houston, Texas,
June 14, 1951

Those who shrug this off (the abolition of war) as idealistic are the real enemies of peace - the real war mongers.

Massachusetts Legislature,
Boston, Massachusetts,
July 25, 1951

Public morality is the touchstone to the people's faith in the integrity of the government process.

Letter to Japanese Prime Minister,
August 20, 1951

(Referring to Korea) What a complete callousness to human feeling and soldier dignity!

National Convention, The American Legion,
Miami, Florida,
October 17, 1951

...the Asian peoples covet the right to shape their own free destiny.

U.S. Congress,
Washington, DC,
April 19, 1951

We must clearly understand that despite our great reservoir of spiritual and material strength we must carefully guard the fundamental basis which produced them. For the drift away from our competitive system of free enterprise is threatening the initiative and incentive of our people and throttling the energies essential to maintain the level of our material progress. The drift away from the truth is leaving the people confused and bewildered. The drift away from those high principles and moral standards from which were evolved the American tradition is creating doubt and uncertainty and lowering the moral tone of the American way of life. The drift downward of the purchasing power of our currency which has progressively fallen as it has become increasingly influenced by the political fortunes of the moment continues unabated. The drift upward in the cost of bureaucracy and the expenditure of public funds in complete disregard of the tax burden has accelerated so alarmingly that the people are rapidly becoming the servants of the State. The drift toward Socialism through indirect internal pressures faces us with the inevitable collapse of individual incentive and full personal energy. This leaves the public safeguard in the direct hands of the American people in whom rests constitutionally the ultimate power to rule. Time and the course of events require that every citizen do his full part in this essential undertaking.

Fort Worth, Texas,
June 16, 1951

We must finally come to realize that war is outmoded as an instrument of political policy, that it provides no solution for international problems; that it but threatens the participants with mutual national suicide.

Massachusetts Legislature,
Boston, Massachusetts,
July 25, 1951

Since my return from service abroad I have enjoyed the privilege, the freedom and the opportunities of private citizenship. I have seen many new and wonderful things but some which to me create a disturbing outlook for the future. Possibly one of the most pernicious is our steady drift toward totalitarian rule with the suppression of those personal liberties which have formed the foundation stones to our political, economic and social advance to national greatness.

Our government now differs substantially from the design of our forefathers as lad down in the Constitution. They envisaged a federation of sovereign states with only such limited power resting in the federal authority as became necessary to serve the common interests of all.

But under the stress of national emergencies during the past two decades, there has been a persistent and progressive centralization of power in the Federal Government with only superficial restoration to the States and the people as emergencies subsided. This drift has resulted in an increasingly dangerous paternalistic relationship between Federal Government and private citizen, with the mushrooming of agency after agency designed to control the individual.

Authority specifically reserved to the States by constitutional mandate has been ignored in the ravenous effort to further centralize the political power. Within the Federal Government itself there has been a further and dangerous centralization.

For example, the Department of State, originally established for the sole purpose of the conduct of foreign diplomacy, has become in effect a general operating agency of government, exercising authority and influence over many facets of executive administration formerly reserved to the President or the heads of other departments. The Department of State indeed is rapidly assuming the character of a Prime Ministry, notwithstanding that its Secretary is an appointed official, neither chosen by nor answerable directly to the people.

This drift toward totalitarian rule is reflected not only in this shift toward centralized power, but as well in the violent manner in which exception is taken to the citizen's voice when raised in criticism of those who exercise the political power.

There seems to be an determination to suppress individual voice and opinion, which can only be regarded as symptomatic of the beginning of a general trend toward mass thought control. Abusive language and arbitrary action, rather than calm, dispassionate and just argument, ill becomes the leadership of a great nation conceived in liberty and dedicated to a course of morality and justice. It challenges the concept of free speech and is an attempt at direct suppression through intimidation of that most vital check against the abuse of political power - public criticism.

If long countenanced by free men, it can but lead to those controls upon conviction and conscience which traditionally have formed stepping stones to dictatorial power.

Cleveland, Ohio,
September 6, 1951

...give primary concern to our own security and the well being of our own people; ...avoid distributing our wealth for the purpose of buying the loyalty of others, or of sharing with others the wealth and security which we hold in sacred trust for our progeny;...

National Convention, The American Legion,
Miami, Florida,
October 17, 1951

Possibly in Asia, where the record is more fully developed and events themselves have more plainly written the judgment, has the irresponsibility of our national policy been more pronounced. There our betrayal of China will ever stand as a black mark upon our escutcheon. But the tragedy of Korea comes closer to the hearts of the American people. For there thousands of our beloved dead give mute evidence to the tragic failure of American leadership.

Mississippi Legislature,
Jackson, Mississippi,
March 22, 1952

Spiritually and physically we possess the resource, properly conserved and realistically applied, to lead toward a world freed from the exhausting wars which have so plagued the past. This is a practical purpose, not visionary. For the destructiveness of modern war has now in the atomic age become too frightful to contemplate by even a potential victor.

Keynote Address,
Republic National Convention,
Chicago, Illinois,
July 7, 1952

It is not of any external threat that I concern myself but rather of insidious forces working from within which have already so drastically altered the character of our free institutions - those institutions which formerly we hailed as something beyond question or challenge - those institutions we proudly called the American way of life.

Massachusetts Legislature,
Boston, Massachusetts,
July 25, 1951

While Asia is commonly referred to as the gateway to Europe, it is no less true that Europe is the gateway to Asia, and the broad influence of the one cannot fail to have its impact upon the other.

U. S. Congress,
Washington, DC,
April 19, 1951

To the early pioneer the Pacific coast marked the end of his courageous westerly advance - to us it should mark but the beginning. To him it delimited our western frontier - to us that frontier has been moved beyond the Pacific horizon. For we find our western defense geared to an Island chain off the coast of continental Asia from which with air and sea supremacy we can dominate any predatory move threatening the Pacific Ocean area.

Opening, Centennial Celebration,
Seattle, Washington,
November 13, 1951

Under such conditions the Pacific no longer represents menacing avenues of approach for a prospective invader - it assumes instead the friendly aspect of a peaceful lake. Our line of defense is a natural one and can be maintained with a minimum of military effort and expense. It envisions no attack against anyone nor does it provide the bastions essential for offensive operations, but properly maintained would be an invincible defense against aggression.

The holding of this littoral defense line in the western Pacific is entirely dependent upon holding all segments thereof, for any major breach of that line by an unfriendly power would render vulnerable to determined attack every other major segment. This is a military estimate as to which I have yet to find a military leader who will take exception. For that reason I have strongly recommended in the pat as a matter of military urgency that under no circumstances must Formosa fall under communist control. Such an eventuality would at once threaten the freedom of the Philippines and the loss of Japan, and might well force our western frontier back to the coasts of California, Oregon and Washington.

U. S. Congress,
Washington, DC,
April 19, 1951

Could there by anything more discouraging and shocking to our soldiers on the line than the deprecating reference to their fierce and savage struggle as a "police action?" Could anything be more agonizing to the mothers of their dead than the belittling reference to it by the Joint Chiefs of Staff as the "Korean skirmish?" What a lack of perspective! What a failure to place first things first! What a complete callousness to human feeling and soldier dignity!

National Convention, The American Legion,
Miami, Florida,
October 17, 1951

How fantastically unrealistic it is for them to refuse to accept the factuality that we are already at war - a bitter, savage and costly war.

Dallas, Texas,
June 15, 1951

Yet, since the end of the Second World War, without committing a single soldier to battle, the Soviet, aided by our own political blunders, has gained a dominion over territory and peoples without parallel in all history - a dominion which it will take years for it to assimilate and administer.

National Convention, The American Legion,
Miami, Florida,
October 17, 1951

In every war in which we have heretofore engaged, we have counter-balanced manpower with the doctrine of attack through our matchless scientific development. Yet, in Korea, we are admittedly applying the doctrine of passive defense which in all history has never won a war - a doctrine which has been responsible for more military disaster than all other reasons combined. Does experience teach us nothing? Has shifting expediency replaced logical reasoning?

Texas Legislature,
Austin, Texas,
June 13, 1951

It might well mean foreclosure upon the chances the Chinese may have had to throw off the chains of Red tyranny and oppression. It perhaps will even mean the ultimate fulfillment of the Russian dream of centuries to secure warm-water outlets to the south as a means of gaining a military posture of global omnipotence, with the hope of ultimate domination over the seaborne commerce of the world. Beyond Asia, Africa would then be exposed to Communist hordes dominating the Indian Ocean area and Europe would come under a real threat of invasion.

Mississippi Legislature,
Jackson, Mississippi,
March 22, 1952

Prejudiced and willful voices scoffed at this warning, but there is where the Communists elected to challenge our spiritual and military strength and there is where we have failed adequately to meet the challenge, even though we had the military resource and means at our command.

Our failure has been of the spirit, not of the arms - a bankruptcy of leadership in our American tradition. Yet this failure has furnished the Soviet the passkey to world conquest. Small wonder that such weakness and vacillation should cause us loss of faith and respect abroad. Not since the early days of the Republic has our nation been so reduced in the universal esteem. Never have we as a people been held in such doubt by others.

Mississippi Legislature,
Jackson, Mississippi,
March 22, 1952

Now that the fighting has temporarily abated the outstanding impression which emerges from the scene is the utter uselessness of the enormous sacrifice in life and limb which has resulted. A million soldier on both sides and unquestionably at least a like number of civilians are maimed or dead. A nation has been gutted and we stand today just where we stood before it all started. The threat of aggression upon the weak by these callously inclined among the strong has not diminished. Indeed nothing has been settled. No issue has been decided.

Massachusetts Legislature,
Boston, Massachusetts,
July 25, 1951

No words can excuse or relieve the enormous disaster to the Korean people we are pledged to protect...

The protection we offer these unfortunate people, indeed may well resolve itself into their complete obliteration. To what greater depths might morality possibly sink?

Mighty efforts are underway to conceal these facts. But the march of events and the common sense of the American people cannot fail ultimately to reveal the full truth.

Texas Legislature,
Austin, Texas,
June 13, 1951

Two great questions about Korea still remain unanswered. First, why did they start the war if they did not intend to win it? And second, what do they intend to do now - go on piling up our dead indefinitely with no fixed purpose or end in sight?

Hardened old soldier though I am - my very soul revolts at this unnecessary slaughter...

National Convention, The American Legion,
Miami, Florida,
October 17, 1951

MacArthur signs the Japanese surrender documents, September 1945.

Six years ago with a few strokes of the pen a calm descended upon the battlefields of the world and the guns grew silent. Military victory had been achieved for our cause and men turned their thoughts from the task of mass killing to the higher duty of international restoration, from destroying to rebuilding, from destruction to construction.

Everywhere in the free world they lifted up their heads and hearts in thanksgiving for the advent of a peace in which ethics and morality, based upon truth and justice, might thereafter fashion the universal code.

Then more than ever in the history of the modern world, a materially strong and spiritually vibrant leadership was needed to consolidate the victory into a truly enduring peace for all of the human race. America, at the very apex of her military power, was the logical nation to which the world turned for such leadership.

It was a crucial moment - one of the greatest opportunities ever known. But our political and military leaders failed to comprehend it.

Sensitive only to the expediencies of the hour, they dissipated with reckless haste that predominant military power which was the key to the situation. Our forces were rapidly and completely demobilized and the great stores of war material which had been accumulated were disposed of with irresponsible waste and abandon.

The world was then left exposed and vulnerable to an international Communism whose long publicized plan had been to await just such a favorable opportunity to establish dominion over the free nations. The stage had perhaps been unwittingly set in secret and most unfortunate war conferences.

Cleveland, Ohio,
September 6, 1951

Our great military victory has been offset, largely because of military unpreparedness, by the political successes of the Kremlin.

Cleveland, Ohio,
September 6, 1951

Our diplomatic blunders increased as our senseless disarmament became a reality. And now the disastrous cycle is completed as those same leaders who lost to the world the one great chance it has had for enduring universal peace, frantically endeavor, by arousing a frenzy of fear throughout the land, to gear anew our energies and resources, to rebuild our dissipated strength and to face again a future of total war.

Our need for adequate military defense, with world tensions as they were and are, is and should have been completely evident even before the end of the war.

Cleveland, Ohio,
September 6, 1951

I recall so vividly the American Legion's warning to the country at the close of the war some 6 years ago. Its resolution read as follows:

"...the only present guarantee of our nation's safety and freedom and the best presently available assurance of world peace is to have in the hands of this great peace-loving Nation the mightiest armament in the world."

Sound and far-sighted advice which considered the present and drew upon the lessons and experience of the past. Had it been heeded by our political and military leaders, we would have been able to consolidate our great moral and military victory and lead the world to an enduring peace. We would not now be frantically endeavoring to restore our dissipated military strength. The Soviet would be but a negative influence upon world affairs and the earth would be a much gentler place on which to live. But our leaders failed to heed that advice.

They failed to recognize the opportunity for leadership which victory had cast. They failed to see the enormity of the Communist threat to an impoverished postwar world.

National Convention, The American Legion,
Miami, Florida,
October 17, 1951

I should be recreant, moreover, to my obligations of citizenship did I fail to warn that the policies of appeasement on which we are now embarked carry within themselves the very incitation to war against us. If the Soviet does strike it will be because of the weakness we now display rather than the strength we of right should display.

Texas Legislature,
Austin, Texas,
June 13, 1951

If, however, we be so weak in fact that we must cower before the verbal brandishments of others, the responsibility for such weakness should be a matter of the gravest public concern.

Who, we should ask, is responsible for the reduction of our military strength from the greatest on earth at war's end to that they now estimate is inadequate even to support our moral commitment?

Who plunged us into the Korean war and assumed other global commitments in the face of such alleged weakness, without reckoning and being ready to meet their potential consequence? Who is responsible for so grave a past failure which has brought our nation to so ignominious a pass that we must plead weakness before our fellow nations?

Texas Legislature,
Austin, Texas,
June 13, 1951

It is not from threat of external attack that we have reason for fear. It is from those insidious forces working from within. It is they that create the basis for fear by spreading false propaganda designed to destroy those moral precepts to which we have clung for direction since the immutable Declaration of Independence became the great charter of our liberty.

This campaign to pervert the truth and shape or confuse the public mind with its consequent weakening of moral courage is not chargeable entirely to Communists engaged in a centrally controlled world wide conspiracy to destroy all freedom. For they have many allies, here as elsewhere who, blind to reality, ardently support the general Communist aims while reacting violently to the mere suggestion that they do so.

Flag Day,
Houston, Texas,
June 14, 1951

There are those who seek to subvert government from being the guardian of the people's rights, to make of it an instrument of despotic power.

Flag Day,
Houston, Texas,
June 14, 1951

What, I have been asked, is our greatest internal menace? If I were permitted but one sentence of reply, but one phrase of warning - it would be - end invisible government based upon propaganda and restore truly representative government based upon truth.

For propaganda is the primary instrument of totalitarian rule, whether Communist or Fascist, and, incredible as it may seem to those of my generation, it is practiced as though it were a legitimate art or science. Suppress the truth, curtail free expression and you destroy the basis of all the freedoms.

San Antonio, Texas,
June 15, 1951

The potentiality of America's industrial strength in support of our expanding armament is guarantee against the wilfully designed military action against us.

But wars can come about through blundering statesmanship animated by a lust for political power. Our course can and must be designed to promote the peace.

Opening, Centennial Celebration,
Seattle, Washington,
November 13, 1951

I hesitate to refer to my own relief from the Far Eastern Commands as I have never questioned the legal authority underlying such action. But the three sole reasons publicly stated by the highest authority clearly demonstrate the arbitrary nature of the decision.

The first reason given was that, contrary to existing policy, I warned of the strategic relationship of Formosa to American security and the dangers inherent in this area's falling under Communist control. Yet this viewpoint has since been declared by the Secretary of State, under oath before Congressional Committees, to have been and to be the invincible and long standing policy of the United States.

The second reason given was that I communicated my readiness to meet the enemy commander at any time to discuss acceptable terms of a cease fire arrangement. Yet, for this proposal, I was relieved of my command by the same authorities who since have received so enthusiastically the identical proposal when made by the Soviet Government.

The third and final reason advanced was my replying to a Congressman's request for information on the public subject then under open consideration by the Congress. Yet both Houses of Congress promptly passed a law confirming my action, which indeed had been entirely in accordance with a long existing and well recognized though unwritten policy.

This law states that no member of the Armed Forces shall be restricted or prevented from communicating directly or indirectly with any member of members of Congress concerning any subject, unless such communication is in violation of law or the security and safety of the United States. And this formal enactment of basic public policy was approved without the slightest dissent of the President.

Is there wonder that men who seek an objective understanding of American policy thinking become completely frustrated and bewildered? Is there wonder that Soviet propaganda so completely dominates American foreign policy?

Massachusetts Legislature,
Boston, Massachusetts,
July 25, 1951

The American Legion, composed of men who know the detest war for the scourge that it is, is peculiarly well fitted to stand guard over our heritage of American liberty. It must exercise unrelaxed vigilance. It must ensure that neither political expediency nor foreign infatuation influences the expenditure of the vast sums now under contemplation for freedom's defense.

It must exercise its great influence to the end that: we rearm - as rearm we must - in an atmosphere of confidence in our inherent strength, not under the hysteria of an artificially created fear;

That it is our implacable purpose to retain undisputed control of the seas, to secure undisputed control of the air, to vigorously implement our atomic program with a full commitment to the use as needed of the atomic weapon, and while maintaining a well-balanced and highly developed ground force, to charge to our allies the main responsibility for ground operations in defense of their own spheres of territorial interest;

To curb the growing tendency of political and military leaders to publicize for political advantage classified data concerning scientific developments incident to our military effort, and thus to yield the all important element of surprise;

To do all reasonably within our power to help preserve freedom for those who have the will and determination to do all in their power to defend their own freedom;

To avoid being drawn into unreasonable and unnecessary expenditures for armament to create an artificial domestic prosperity for political ends;

To avoid contributing the fruits of our system of free enterprise to support Socialism or Communism abroad under the spurious pretense that it serves our own military security;

To avoid aligning ourselves with colonial policies in Asia and the Middle East, lest we invite the enmity of the traditionally friendly peoples of those vast areas of the world;

To give primary concern to our own security and the well being of our own people;

To avoid distributing our wealth for the purpose of buying the loyalty of others, or of sharing with others the wealth and security which we hold in sacred trust for our progeny;

To apply all possible pressure, short of war, upon the Soviet or any associated power which by abuse and pressure upon us forces the expenditure of such vast outlays of our energy and resources as a measure of self-preservation;

To avoid a protracted and indecisive war in Korea with its endless slaughter - the Chief of Staff of the Army recently testified before a Congressional Committee that it might last for ten years;

To regain military faith in ourselves and the policies upon which our victories in past have always rested;

To do all reasonably within our power to assist the Filipino and Japanese people to advance and fortify their liberties and the Chinese people to regain theirs;

And, above all else, to preserve inviolate those great principles and ideals of moral authority upon which is based the American way of life and the nobility of the cause for which our soldier fight.

National Convention, The American Legion,
Miami, Florida,
October 17, 1951

Every nation that has what is valuable is obligated to be prepared to defend against brutal attack or unjust effort to seize and appropriate.

Veterans of The Rainbow (42nd) Infantry
Division of World War I,
Washington, DC,
July 14, 1935

Every nation that would preserve its tranquility, its riches, its independence, and its self-respect must keep alive its martial order and be at all time prepared to defend itself.

Veterans of The Rainbow (42nd) Infantry
Division of World War I,
Washington, DC,
July 14, 1935

Our first line of defense for Western Europe is not the Elbe; it is not the Rhine - it is the Yalu.

Texas Legislature
Austin, Texas,
June 13, 1951

We have indeed reached an astounding concept of morality when an official estimate such as that put out in December 1949 on Formosa, is now stated to be false and to have been intentionally publicized in order to mislead public opinion.

San Antonio, Texas,
June 15, 1951

MacArthur rides in a New York City parade, April 1951.

RELIGION

Into the ensuing spiritual vacuum flowed the American concept of honor and justice and compassion drawn from our Christian teachings.

National Institute of Social Sciences,
Annual Dinner,
Waldorf-Astoria Hotel, New York, New York,
November 8, 1951

The people have it in their hands to restore morality, wisdom and vision to the direction of our foreign and domestic affairs and regain the religious base which in times past assured general integrity in public and private life.

Opening, Centennial Celebration,
Seattle, Washington,
November 13, 1951

...there is unmistakable evidence of a tendency toward moral deterioration throughout the free world.

Texas Legislature,
Austin, Texas,
June 13, 1951

I warned of the need for "a spiritual recrudescence and improvement of human character that will synchronize with our almost matchless advances in science, art, literature and material and cultural development."

U.S. Congress,
Washington, DC,
April 19, 1951

The problem basically is theological and involves a spiritual recrudescence and improvement of human character that will synchronize with our almost matchless advances in science, art, literature and all material and cultural developments ...

V J Day Broadcast, U.S.S. Missouri,
Tokyo Bay,
September 2, 1945

Our own people harbor a strong spiritual urge in their hearts, but many leaders have become absorbed in the demands of political expediency, are not unwilling to compromise moral principals and have lost the traditional American patriot's touch.

Texas Legislature,
Austin, Texas,
June 13, 1951

...is the deep spiritual urge in the hearts of our people... capable of arousing and directing a decisive and impelling public opinion.

Flag Day,
Houston, Texas,
June 14, 1951

It (spiritual urge) is an infallible reminder that our greatest hope and faith rests upon two mighty symbols - the Cross and the Flag.

Flag Day,
Houston, Texas,
June 14, 1951

It (our Nation) was never more able to meet the exacting tests of leadership in peace or in war, spiritually, physically or materially. As it is yet unconquered, so is it unconquerable. Its history still lies ahead. Our finest hours are yet to come.

Texas Legislature,
Austin, Texas,
June 13, 1951

...the only road, to universal peace and prosperity. We must lead the world down that road however long and tortuous and illusory it may now appear.

Massachusetts Legislature,
Boston, Massachusetts,
July 25, 1951

Are we going to preserve the religious base to our origin, our growth and our progress or yield to the devious assaults of atheistic or other anti-religious forces?

Cleveland, Ohio,
September 6, 1951

In short, is American life of the future to be characterized by freedom or by servitude, strength or weakness? The answer must be clear and unequivocal if we are to avoid the pitfalls toward which we are heading with such certainty. In many respects it is not to be found in any dogma of political philosophy but in those immutable precepts which underlie the Ten Commandments.

Cleveland, Ohio,
September 6, 1951

The people have it in their hands to restore morality, wisdom and vision to the direction of our foreign and domestic affairs and regain the religious base which in times past assured general integrity in public and private life.

Opening, Centennial Celebration,
Seattle, Washington,
November 13, 1951.

A Christian nation, the Philippines stand as a mighty bulwark of Christianity in the Far East, and its capacity for high moral leadership in Asia is unlimited.

U. S. Congress,
Washington, DC,
April 19, 1951

On September 2nd, 1945, after taking the surrender of Japan in Tokyo Bay, I warned of the need for a "spiritual recrudescence and improvement of human character that will synchronize with our almost matchless advances in science, art, literature and material and cultural development." Such an improvement is slow to come to pass. To the contrary, there is unmistakable evidence of a tendency toward moral deterioration throughout the free world. This moral deterioration does not occur through evolutionary change in human thought but rather from the relentless war being waged by a fifth column within the ranks of every free society. This is a far greater threat to the free world than is the advance of predatory force. Its very purpose is to destroy faith in moral values, to introduce cynicism in human thought and the transform tranquility into confusion, disorder and dismay. Our own people harbor a strong spiritual urge in their hearts, but many leaders have become absorbed in the demands of political expediency, are not unwilling to compromise moral principle and have lost the traditional American patriot's touch. Such a leadership offers no panacea for freedom's festering wounds.

Texas Legislature,
Austin, Texas,
June 13, 1951

On this day (Flag Day) annually set apart for all Americans to re-pledge their allegiance to the Flag and to the Republic for which it stands let us pray for the spiritual strength and innate wisdom to keep this nation to the course of freedom charted by our fathers; to preserve it as the mighty instrument on earth to bring universal order out of existing chaos; to restore liberty where liberty has perished; and to reestablish human dignity where dignity has been suppressed.

Flag Day,
Houston, Texas,
June 14, 1951

Our need for patriotic fervor and religious devotion was never more impelling.

Massachusetts Legislature,
Boston, Massachusetts,
July 25, 1951

I do not know the dignity of the birth of these men but I do know the glory of their death. They died that our nation might live in freedom. Their memory should be held immortal and a merciful God will rest their souls.

Waltham, Massachusetts,
July 26, 1951

...the spiritual impulse is strong in many American hearts and constitutes a rugged bulwark in the defense of religious morality against any advance of atheistic immorality.

Salvation Army,
Waldorf-Astoria Hotel, New York, New York,
December 12, 1951

We must refuse to indulge those who are so blind they will not see the moral dangers now threatening the engulfment of our people. We must regain our spiritual and intellectual balance that there may be restored a full faith in public integrity and a renewed devotion to private morality. We must face the gravity of the times honestly and fearlessly so that our beloved country may survive the man-made periods which now confront it.

Salvation Army,
Waldorf-Astoria Hotel, New York, New York,
December 12, 1951

Our great strength rests in those high-minded and patriotic Americans whose faith in God and love of country transcends all selfish and self-serving instincts.

Salvation Army,
Waldorf-Astoria Hotel, New York, New York,
December 12, 1951

Words can but inadequately portray the deep sentiment which stirs my heart as I revisit this scene of my birth. I have just come from Christ Church where my beloved parents - a lovely lady of the South and a distinguished soldier of the North - first dedicated me through baptism to the service of God. My emotions are too deep for attempted utterance. I can but offer you the humble gratitude of a native son for the devoted care with which you have preserved this building. In my eyes it is hallowed for its memory of my sainted mother as she gave me the distinction of southern birth. I offer you, too, my thanks for the unfailing confidence and support you have given me throughout the years of my absence in the service of our country. I have drawn strength and inspiration from it during many, lonely and difficult moments of doubt and decision.

MacArthur Park,
Little Rock, Arkansas,
March 23, 1952

....remember what Thomas Jefferson said, "The Bible is the cornerstone of liberty."

Michigan Legislature,
Lansing, Michigan,
May 15, 1952

Our need for patriotic fervor and religious devotion was never more impelling. There can be no compromise with atheistic communism - no half-way in the preservation of freedom and religion.

Massachusetts Legislature,
Boston, Massachusetts,
July 25, 1951

For as Daniel Webster once said: "If we abide by the principles taught in the Bible, our country will prosper and go on prospering; but, if we and our posterity neglect its instructions and authority, no man can tell how suddenly a catastrophe may overwhelm us, and bury all our glory in profound obscurity."

Michigan Legislature,
Lansing, Michigan,
May 15, 1952

The religious devotion of the American people which has produced the universally reflected spirituality of the American home has been outraged by the materialism and selfishness which dominates the national administration. Public policy no longer is geared to the simple determination of that which is right and that which is wrong. The objective has been to build political strength even at the expense of the public interest. This is incomprehensible to our people who understand fully the influence religion and morality have always exerted upon political stability. They know from the lessons of history that national strength and greatness inevitably find their true measure in existing moral and ethical standards.

Keynote Address,
Republic National Convention,
Chicago, Illinois,
July 7, 1952

The springs of human conflict cannot be eradicated through institutions but only through the reform of the individual human being. And that is a task which has baffled the highest theologians for 2,000 years and more.

Veterans of the Rainbow (42nd) Infantry
Division of World War I,
Washington, DC,
July 14, 1935

We all dream of the day when human conduct will be governed by the Decalogue and the Sermon on the Mount.

Veterans of the Rainbow (42nd) Infantry
Division of World War I,
Washington, DC,
July 14, 1935

The soldier, above all men, is required to perform the highest act of religious teaching - sacrifice.

Accepting the baton of Field Marshall,
Malacanan Palace, Philippines,
August 24, 1936

The soldier, above all other men, is required to practice the greatest act of religious training - sacrifice.

U. S. Military Academy,
West Point, New York,
May 12, 1962

In this day of gathering storms, as the moral deterioration of political power spreads its growing infection, it is essential that every spiritual force be mobilized to defend and preserve the religious base upon which this nation was founded. For ti is that base which has bee the motivating impulse to our moral and national growth. History fails to record a single precedent in which nations subject to moral decay have not passed into political and economic decline. There has been either a spiritual reawakening to overcome the moral lapse, or a progressive deterioration leading to ultimate national disaster.

Salvation Army,
Waldorf-Astoria Hotel, New York, New York,
December 12, 1951

In many parts of the world, ancient religions have given way before the sweep of this concept of materialism which holds to the sanctity of no moral law and worships as its only god the power to suppress the Divine heritage of man. It first essays to make traitors among those of high degree and through them seeks to destroy nations and bend peoples to its malevolent will.

Salvation Army,
Waldorf-Astoria Hotel, New York, New York,
December 12, 1951

I shall continue to fight against that greatest scourge of mankind, Communism, as long as God gives me the power to fight. I shall work with you in the discharge of our common responsibilities of citizenship to the end that American policy be based upon the thoughts and needs and aspirations of the American people, unyielding to undue political pressures from abroad. I shall stand with you for an America rededicated to those sacred and immutable ideals and concepts which guided our forefathers when drawing the design of American freedom.

Chicago, Illinois,
April 26, 1951

There are those who seek to convert us to a form of socialistic endeavor leading directly to the path of Communist slavery. As a counter-balance to those forces is the deep spiritual urge in the hearts of our people - a spiritual urge capable of arousing and directing a decisive and impelling public opinion. This, indeed is the great safeguard and resource of America. So long as it exists we are secure for it holds us to the path of reason. It is an infallible reminder that our greatest hope and faith rests upon two mighty symbols - the Cross and the Flag; the one based upon those immutable teachings which provide the spiritual strength to persevere along the course which is just and right - the other based upon the invincible will that human freedom shall not perish from the earth. These are the mighty bulwarks against the advance of those atheistic predatory forces which seek to destroy the spirituality of the human mind and to enslave the human body.

Flag Day,
Houston, Texas,
June 14, 1951

The issues which today confront the nation are clearly defined and so fundamental as to directly involve the very survival of the Republic.

Are we going to preserve the religious base to our origin, our growth and our progress or yield to the devious assaults of atheistic or other anti-religious forces?

Are we going to maintain our present course toward State Socialism with Communism just beyond or reverse the present trend and regain our hold upon our heritage of liberty and freedom?

Are we going to squander our limited resources to the point of our own inevitable exhaustion or adopt commonsense policies of frugality which will insure financial stability in our time and a worth-while heritage in that of our progeny?

Are we going to continue to yield personal liberties and community autonomy to the steady and inexplorable centralization of all political power or restore the Republic to constitutional direction, regain our personal liberties and reassume the individual State's primary responsibility and authority in the conduct of local affairs?

Are we going to permit a continuing decline in public and private morality of re-establish high ethical standards as the means of regaining a diminishing faith in the integrity of our public and private institutions?

Are we going to continue to permit the pressure of alien doctrines to strongly influence the orientation of foreign and domestic policy or regain trust in our own traditions, experience and free institutions and the wisdom or our own people?

In short, is American life of the future to be characterized by freedom or by servitude, strength or weakness. The answer must be clear and unequivocal if we are to avoid the pitfalls toward which we are now heading with such certainty. In many respects it is not to be found in any dogma of political philosophy but in those immutable precepts which underlay the Ten Commandments.

Cleveland, Ohio,
September 6, 1951

THE SOLDIER

They (duty, honor, country) mold you for your future roles as the custodians of the Nation's defense.

U. S. Military Academy,
West Point, New York,
May 12, 1962

It (the military code) embraces the highest moral laws.

Veterans of The Rainbow (42nd) Infantry
Division of World War I,
Washington, DC,
July 14, 1935

Learn to laugh yet never forget how to weep.

101st Commencement, Michigan State Univ.,,
Lansing, Michigan,
June 11, 1961

Be modest so that you will remember the simplicity of true greatness, the open mind of true wisdom.

U. S. Military Academy,
West Point, New York,
May 12, 1962

The long gray line has never failed us.

U. S. Military Academy,
West Point, New York,
May 12, 1962

...the soldier above all other people prays for peace for he must suffer and bear the deepest wounds and scars of war.

U. S. Military Academy,
West Point, New York,
May 12, 1962

The soldier, above all other men, is required to perform the highest act of religious teaching - sacrifice.

Veterans of The Rainbow (42nd) Infantry
Division of World War I,
Washington, DC,
July 14, 1935

The soldier, above all other men, is required to perform the highest act of religious training - sacrifice.

U. S. Military Academy,
West Point, New York,
May 12, 1962

To reach into the future yet never neglect the past.

101st Commencement, Michigan State Univ.,,
Lansing, Michigan,
June 11, 1961

... the soldier who is called upon to offer and to give his life for his country is the noblest development of mankind.

Veterans of The Rainbow (42nd) Infantry
Division of World War I,
Washington, DC,
July 14, 1935

(On Soldiers in battle) I do not know the dignity of their birth, but I do know the glory of their death.

Veterans of The Rainbow (42nd) Infantry
Division of World War I,
Washington, DC,
July 14, 1935

I regard him (the American soldier) now as one of the worlds noblest figures, not only as one of the finest military characters, but also one of the most stainless.

U. S. Military Academy,
West Point, New York,
May 12, 1962

Old soldiers never die, they just fade away

City Hall,
San Francisco, California,
April 18, 1951

However horrible the incidents of war may be, the soldier who is called upon to offer and give his life for his country is the noblest development of mankind. (This expression which MacArthur used on many occasions was called "the Apostle's creed of MacArthurism".)

Accepting the baton of Field Marshall,
Malacanan Palace, Philippines,
August 24, 1936

It (this magnificent monument) will be a fitting tribute to the valor and sacrifice of the American soldier.

Milwaukee, Wisconsin,
April 27, 1951

No fraternity of men ever rested upon a more noble concept than does the American Legion.

National Convention, The American Legion,
Miami, Florida,
October 17, 1951

...I still remember the refrain of one of the most popular barrack ballads of that day (day he took the oath at West Point) which proclaimed most proudly that: "Old soldiers never die - they just fade away." And like the old soldier of that ballad, I now close my military career and just fade away - an old soldier who tired to do his duty as God gave him the light to see that duty.

U. S. Congress,
Washington, DC,
April 19, 1951

It is difficult to ask men to fight and die unless we give them a realistic mission and means to accomplish it.

Chicago, Illinois,
April 26, 1951

I am profoundly grateful for the opportunity to participate in the dedication of this magnificent monument. It will be a fitting tribute to the valor and sacrifice of the American soldier. Its full glory will be an imperishable reminder to all mankind of those deeds which preserved our liberties on the battlefields of the world. It stands as solemn warning to those who would destroy freedom, either externally or internally. America will not now nor in future yield that for which so many of these men died. I do not know the dignity of their birth, but I do know the glory of their death. They died that mortal ideals might not perish. This monument will do even more than commemorate them. It will serve to rally all Americans to the task of maintaining the moral strength which has built our past. It will constantly remind of those sacred and immutable concepts - liberty, justice and truth - upon which long has rested the Republic's fate. It will be for all eyes and for all time a symbol of an ever stronger nation whose history still is the future.

Milwaukee, Wisconsin,
April 27, 1951

...I find in existence a new and heretofore unknown and dangerous concept that the members of our armed forces owe primary allegiance and loyalty to those who temporarily exercise the authority of the executive branch of government, rather than to the country and its constitution which they are sworn to defend. No proposition could be more dangerous.

Massachusetts Legislature,
Boston, Massachusetts,
July 25, 1951

I am deeply grateful for this opportunity to address those who brought victory to American arms in the past two great wars of world history. I do so as a member of this Legion holding no public office, advocating no partisan cause and animated by the sole desire to help restore, preserve and advance those great American principles and ideals of which we have been beneficiaries ourselves and are now trustees for future American generations.

National Convention, The American Legion,
Miami, Florida,
October 17, 1951

Could there be anything more discouraging and shocking to our soldiers on the line than the deprecating reference to their fierce and savage struggle as a "police action"? Could anything be more agonizing to the mothers of their dead than the belittling reference to it by the Joint Chiefs of Staff as the "Korean skirmish"? What a lack of perspective! What a failure to place first thing's first! What a complete callousness to human feeling and soldier dignity! Two great questions about Korea still remain unanswered. First, why did they start the war if they did not intend to win it? And second, what do they intend to do now? - so in piling up our dead indefinitely with no fixed purpose or end in sight? Hardened old soldier though I am - my very soul revolts at this unnecessary slaughter of the flower of our youth.

National Convention, The American Legion,
Miami, Florida,
October 17, 1951

The American Legion, composed of men who know and detest war for the scourge that it is, is peculiarly well fitted to stand guard over our heritage of American liberty.

National Convention, The American Legion,
Miami, Florida,
October 17, 1951

One of the greatest contributions The American Legion has made to the nation has been in the strengthening of the potentialities of the citizen soldier. Since the Minute Men of 1776 formed the ranks of the Continental Army and brought victory to its arms in the American Revolution, the security of the United States has rested more than all else upon the competence, the indomitable will and the resolute patriotism of the citizen soldier. The professional has had his role - and it has been a major one - providing trained leadership, initial security against surprise attack and the nucleus to an expanding force under conditions of national emergency. But in all of our wars, from the Revolution to Korea, the citizen soldier has met the full shock of battle, has contributed all but a fraction of the dead and maimed and has accepted the responsibility for victory.

Article, American Legion Magazine,
January, 1952

It was with you I lived my greatest moment. It is of you that I have my greatest memories.

Veterans of the Rainbow (42nd) Infantry
Division of World War I,
Washington, DC,
July 14, 1935

However horrible the incidents of war may be, the soldier who is called upon to offer and to give his life for his country is the noblest development of mankind.

Veterans of the Rainbow (42nd) Infantry
Division of World War I,
Washington, DC,
July 14, 1935

He (the American soldier) needs no eulogy from me, or from any other man; he has written his own history, and written it in red on his enemy's breast.

U. S. Military Academy,
West Point, New York,
May 12, 1962

...when I think of his patience in adversity, of his courage under fire, and of his modesty in victory, I am filled with an emotion of admiration I cannot put into words.

U. S. Military Academy,
West Point, New York,
May 12, 1962

...when I think of his patience under adversity, of his courage under fire, and of his modesty in victory I am filled with an emotion I cannot express.

Veterans of the Rainbow (42nd) Infantry
Division of World War I,
Washington, DC,
July 14, 1935

Only those are fit to live who are not afraid to die.

Veterans of the Rainbow (42nd) Infantry
Division of World War I,
Washington, DC,
July 14, 1935

In chambered temples of silence the dust of his dauntless valor sleeps, waiting. Waiting in the chancery of Heaven...

Veterans of the Rainbow (42nd) Infantry
Division of World War I,
Washington, DC,
July 14, 1935

By praising them when they were good and shaming them when they were bad, by raising their pride and developing their sense of self-respect, I soon began to convince them they were the best of the lot.

General of the Army Douglas MacArthur
"Reminiscences"
McGraw-Hill Book Company, New York, 1964

The military code which he (the American soldier) perpetuates has come down to us from even before the age of knighthood and chivalry. It ... will stand the test of any ethics or philosophies ...

Veterans of the Rainbow (42nd) Infantry
Division of World War I,
Washington, DC,
July 14, 1935

He (the American soldier) belongs to posterity as the instructor of future generations in the principles of liberty and right.

Veterans of the Rainbow (42nd) Infantry
Division of World War I,
Washington, DC,
July 14, 1935

History teaches, too, that almost every military occupation breeds new wars of the future.

General of the Army Douglas MacArthur
"Reminiscences"
McGraw-Hill Book Company, New York, 1964

Editor's note: His proudest achievement in World War II was not in his victories but in the small cost of human life with which he achieved them. He insisted that in most battles and campaigns, superior commanders will find some way to avoid frontal attack, in an effort to achieve victory with minimum casualties. In his belief that the military is a noble profession, he insisted upon a high standard of conduct by the soldier and a high sense of responsibility in command. In approving the death sentence passed upon General Yamashita, for example, he wrote:

The soldier, be he friend or foe, is charged with the protection of the weak and the unarmed. It is the very essence and reason for his being. When he violates this sacred trust, he not only profanes his entire cult but threatens the very fabric of international society. The traditions of fighting men are long and honorable. They are based upon the noblest of human traits — sacrifice.

In approving Homma's sentence, he wrote:

The proceedings show the defendant lacked the basic firmness of character and moral fortitude essential to officers charged with the high command of military forces in the field. No nation can safely trust its martial honor to leaders who do not maintain the universal code which distinguishes between those things that are right and those things that are wrong.

"The Oratory of Douglas MacArthur"
Ph.D. dissertation by Armel Dyer
University of Oregon, 1968

That age-old struggle between the civil and the military to fix the exact line of demarcation between executive control and the professional duty of the soldier.

General of the Army Douglas MacArthur
"Reminiscences"
McGraw-Hill Book Company, New York, 1964

The story of the infantry soldier is an old and honorable one. He carries his home with him - and often his grave. Somehow, he has to bring along the whole paraphernalia of fighting, as well as domesticated living: the grocery store, the ration dump; the hospital, the Medical Corps; the garage, the motor pool; the telephone, the Signal Service. He must sleep and eat and fight and die on foot, in all weather, rain or shine, with or without shelter. He is vulnerable day and night. Death has his finger on him for twenty-four hours, in battle, going toward it, or retreating from it. It is a wonder that the morale of those uniformed gypsies never falters.

General of the Army Douglas MacArthur
"Reminiscences"
McGraw-Hill Book Company, New York, 1964

137

WAR

In war, indeed, there can be no substitute for victory.

U. S. Congress,
Washington, DC,
April 19, 1951

...in war there is no substitute for victory.

U. S. Military Academy,
West Point, New York,
May 12, 1962

Plato quote, "Only the dead have seen the end of war."

U. S. Military Academy,
West Point, New York,
May 12, 1962

Never in history has a nation and its people been more completely crushed than were the Japanese at the end of the struggle.

National Institute of Social Sciences,
Annual Dinner,
Waldorf-Astoria Hotel, New York, New York,
November 8, 1951

The pages of history in recording America's twentieth century contributions to human progress may, perchance, pass over lightly the wars we have fought. But, I believe they will not fail to record the profound influence for good upon Asia which will inevitably follow the spiritual regeneration of Japan.

National Institute of Social Sciences,
Annual Dinner,
Waldorf-Astoria Hotel, New York, New York,
November 8, 1951

He (the American soldier) has written his own history and written it in red on his enemy's breast.

U. S. Military Academy,
West Point, New York,
May 12, 1962

Editor's note: This expression which MacArthur used on many occasions was called "the Apostle's creed of MacArthurism."

However horrible the incidents of war may be, the soldier who is called upon to offer and give his life for his country is the noblest development of mankind.

U. S. Military Academy,
West Point, New York,
May 12, 1962

...and through all this welter of change and development your mission remains fixed, determined, inviolable, it is to win our wars. Everything else in your professional career is but a corollary to this vital dedication.

U. S. Military Academy,
West Point, New York,
May 12, 1962

...diplomatic appeasement but sows the seeds of future conflict. ...we now practice a new and yet more dangerous form of appeasement - appeasement on the battlefield...

Texas Legislature,
Austin, Texas,
June 13, 1951

...in Korea, we are admittedly applying the doctrine of passive defense which in all history has never won a war...

Texas Legislature,
Austin, Texas,
June 13, 1951

Editor's note: During the Luzon campaign in early 1941-42, MacArthur was able to delay the Japanese mass from the use of Manila and Manila Bay for nearly 6 months.

... hold long enough to force the Japanese to deploy in full force, ... slowly give way, leaving the engineers ... to dynamite bridges and construct roadblocks to bar the way. Again and again, these tactics would be repeated. Stand and fight, slip back and dynamite. It was savage and bloody, but it won time.

General of the Army Douglas MacArthur
"Reminiscences"
McGraw-Hill Book Company, New York, 1964

(In desperate military situations when defeat seems imminent.) The subtle corrosion of panic or fatigue or the feeling of just being fed up, can only be arrested by the intervention of the leader. ... in war, to be effective, it must take the form of a fraternity of danger welded between a commander and his troops by the common denominator of sharing the risk of sudden death.

General of the Army Douglas MacArthur
"Reminiscences"
McGraw-Hill Book Company, New York, 1964

...but that's the way it is in war. You win or lose, live or die - and the difference is just an eyelash.

General of the Army Douglas MacArthur
"Reminiscences"
McGraw-Hill Book Company, New York, 1964

Nature is neutral in war, but if you beat it and the enemy does not, it becomes a powerful ally.

General of the Army Douglas MacArthur
"Reminiscences"
McGraw-Hill Book Company, New York, 1964

I could almost hear my father's voice telling me ..., "Doug, councils of war breed timidity and defeatism."

General of the Army Douglas MacArthur
"Reminiscences"
McGraw-Hill Book Company, New York, 1964

What the Australians needed was a strategy that held out the promise of victory.

General of the Army Douglas MacArthur
"Reminiscences"
McGraw-Hill Book Company, New York, 1964

The objective of any warring nation is victory, immediate and complete.

Annual Report of the Chief of Staff,
United States Army,
June 30, 1931

No man in the world is more anxious to avoid the expansion of war than I.

Texas Legislature,
Austin, Texas,
June 13, 1951

I am a 100% disbeliever in war.

Texas Legislature,
Austin, Texas,
June 13, 1951

The enormous sacrifices that have been brought about by scientific methods of killing have rendered war a fantastic and impossible method for the solution of international difficulties.

Texas Legislature,
Austin, Texas,
June 13, 1951

In war, as it is waged now, with the enormous losses on both sides, both will loose. It is a form of mutual suicide...

Milwaukee, Wisconsin,
April 27, 1951

How fantastically unrealistic it is for them to refuse to accept the factuality that we are already at war - a bitter, savage and costly war.

Dallas, Texas,
June 15, 1951

...each war becomes increasingly savage as the means for mass killing are further developed.

Massachusetts Legislature,
Boston, Massachusetts,
July 25, 1951

You cannot control war; you can only abolish it. Those who shrug this off as idealistic are the real enemies of peace - the real war mongers.

Massachusetts Legislature,
Boston, Massachusetts,
July 25, 1951

They died that our nation might live in freedom.

Waltham, Massachusetts,
July 26, 1951

Every distinguished military leader of the past and all military experience from the beginning of time warns this (defense only strategy) but invites failure.

National Convention, The American Legion,
Miami, Florida,
October 17, 1951

Never in history has a nation and its people been more completely crushed than were the Japanese at the end of the struggle.

National Institute of Social Sciences,
Annual Dinner,
Waldorf-Astoria Hotel, New York, New York,
November 8, 1951

The pages of history in recording America's twentieth century contributions to human progress may, perchance, pass over lightly the wars we have fought. But, I believe they will not fail to record the profound influence for good upon Asia which will inevitably follow the spiritual regeneration of Japan.

National Institute of Social Sciences,
Annual Dinner,
Waldorf-Astoria Hotel, New York, New York,
November 8, 1951

There are those who claim our strength is inadequate to protect on both fronts - that we cannot divide our effort. I can think of no greater expression of defeatism. If a potential enemy can divide his strength on two fronts it is for us to counter his effort.

U. S. Congress,
Washington, DC,
April 19, 1951

No amphibious force can be successful without control of the sea lanes an the air over those lanes in its avenue of advance. With naval and air supremac and modest ground elements to defend bases, any major attack from continent Asia toward us or our friends of the Pacific would be doomed to failure.

U. S. Congress,
Washington, DC,
April 19, 1951

The holding of this littoral defense line in the Western Pacific is entirely de pendent upon holding all segments thereof, for any major breach of that line b an unfriendly power would render vulnerable to determined attack every oth major segment. This is a military estimate as to which I have yet to find a mil tary leader who will take exception. For that reason I have strongly recom mended in the past as a matter of military urgency that under no circumstances mu Formosa fall under communist control. Such an eventuality would at once threate the freedom of the Philippines and the loss of Japan, and might well force our Wes ern frontier back to the coasts of California, Oregon and Washington.

U. S. Congress,
Washington, DC,
April 19, 1951

Through these past fifty years, the Chinese people have thus become milit rized in their concepts and in their ideals. They now constitute excellent soldier with competent staffs and commanders. This has produced a new and dominar power in Asia which for its own purposes is allied with Soviet Russia, but wic in its own concepts and methods has become aggressively imperialistic with lust for expansion and increased power normal to this type of imperialism. The is little of the ideological concept either one way or another in the Chinese makeuj

U. S. Congress,
Washington, DC,
April 19, 1951

...I believe that the aggressiveness recently displayed not only in Korea, bu also in Indo-China and Tibet and pointing potentially toward the South, reflec predominantly the same lust for the expansion of power which has animate every would-be conqueror since the beginning of time.

U. S. Congress,
Washington, DC,
April 19, 1951

I sent all four of our occupation divisions to the Korean battlefront withou the slightest qualms as to the effect of the resulting power vacuum upon Japan

U. S. Congress,
Washington, DC,
April 19, 1951

With this brief insight into the surrounding areas I now turn to the Korean conflict. While I was not consulted prior to the President's decision to intervene in support of the Republic of Korea, that decision, from a military standpoint, proved a sound one as we hurled back the invader and decimated his forces. Our victory was complete and our objectives within reach when Red China intervened with numerically superior ground forces. This created a new war and an entirely new situation - a situation not contemplated when our forces were committed against the North Korean invaders - a situation which called for new decisions in the diplomatic sphere to permit the realistic adjustment of military strategy. Such decisions have not been forthcoming. While no man in his right mind would advocate sending our ground forces into continental China and such was never give a thought, the new situation did urgently demand a drastic revision of strategic planning if our political aim was to defeat this new enemy as we had defeated the old.

U. S. Congress,
Washington, DC,
April 19, 1951

I called for reinforcements, but was informed that reinforcements were not available. I made clear that if not permitted to destroy the enemy build-up bases north of the Yalu; if not permitted to utilize the friendly Chinese force of some six hundred thousand men on Formosa; if not permitted to blockade the China coast to prevent the Chinese Reds from getting succor from without; and if there were to be no hope of major reinforcements, the position of the command from the military standpoint forbade victory. We could hold in Korea by constant maneuver and at an approximate area where our supply line advantages were in balance with the supply line disadvantages of the enemy, but we could hope at best for only an indecisive campaign, with its terrible and constant attrition upon our forces if the enemy utilized his full military potential. I have constantly called for the new political decisions essential to a solution. Efforts have been made to distort my position. It has been said that I was in effect a warmonger. Nothing could be further from the truth. I know war as few other men now living know it, and nothing to me is more revolting. I have long advocated its complete abolition as its very destructiveness on both friend and foe has rendered it useless as a means of settling international disputes. Indeed, on the 2nd of September 1945, just following the surrender of the Japanese nation on the battleship Missouri, I formally cautioned as follows:

"Men since the beginning of time have sought peace. Various methods through the ages have been attempted to devise international process to prevent or settle disputes between nations. From the very start, workable methods were found insofar as individual citizens were concerned, but the mechanics of an instrumentality of larger international scope have never been successful. Military alliances, balances of power, Leagues of Nations, all in turn failed, leaving the only path to be by way of the crucible of war. The utter destructiveness of war now blots out this alternative. We have had our last chance. If we will not devise some greater and more equitable system, Armageddon will be at our door. The problem basically is theological and involved a spiritual recrudescence and improvement of human character that will synchronize with our almost matchless advances in science, art, literature and all material and cultural developments of the past two thousand years. It must be of the spirit if we are to save the flesh."

But once war is forced upon us, there is no other alternative than to apply every available means to bring it to a swift end. War's very object is victory - not prolonged indecision. In war, indeed, there can be no substitute for victory.

There are some who for varying reasons would appease Red China. They are blind to history's clear lesson. For history teaches with unmistakable emphasis that appeasement but begets new and bloodier war. It points to no single instance where the end has justified that means - where appeasement has led to more than a sham peace. Like blackmail, it lays the basis for new and successively greater demands, until, as in blackmail, violence becomes the only other alternative. "Why," my soldiers asked of me, "surrender military advantages to an enemy in the field?" I could not answer. Some may say to avoid spread of the conflict into an all-out war with China; others, to avoid Soviet intervention. Neither explanation seems valid. For China is already engaging with the maximum power it can commit and the Soviet will not necessarily mesh its actions with our moves. Like a cobra, any new enemy will more likely strike whenever it feels that the relativity in military or other potential is in its favor on a world-wide basis.

U. S. Congress,
Washington, DC,
April 19, 1951

...history teaches with unmistakable emphasis that appeasement but begets new and bloodier war.

U. S. Congress,
Washington, DC,
April 19, 1951

I have just left your fighting sons in Korea. They have met all tests there and I can report to you without reservation they are splendid in every way. It was my constant effort to preserve them and end this savage conflict honorably and with the least loss of time and a minimum sacrifice of life. Its growing bloodshed has caused me the deepest anguish and anxiety. Those gallant men will remain often in my thoughts and in my prayers always.

U. S. Congress,
Washington, DC,
April 19, 1951

In every war in which we have heretofore engaged, we have counter-balanced manpower with the doctrine of attack through our matchless scientific development. Yet, in Korea, we are admittedly applying the doctrine of passive defense which in all history has never won a war - a doctrine which has been responsible for more military disaster than all other reasons combined. Does experience teach us nothing? Has shifting expediency replaced logical reasoning?

Texas Legislature,
Austin, Texas,
June 13, 1951

144

No man in the world is more anxious to avoid the expansion of war than I. I am a one hundred percent disbeliever in war. The enormous sacrifices that have been brought about by scientific methods of killing have rendered war a fantastic and impossible method for the solution of international difficulties. In war, as it is waged now, with the enormous losses on both sides, both will lose. It is a form of mutual suicide; and I believe that the entire effort of modern society should be concentrated on an endeavor to outlaw it.

This would probably take decades before it could be actually accomplished; but, you have to make a start. There is no half-way substitute. And, the sooner we come to grips with the basic problem the sooner we will reach a solution - it is no more difficult to settle the fundamental issue than it is the various problems that are corollary to it.

The world should have common sense enough, when it surveys the last two wars, to understand that war has become incompatible with the survival of modern civilization. Time is running out on us. We have had our last chance, and I believe firmly that 99 percent of the people of the world agree.

It is the establishment of the mechanics for its abolition that is so difficult. It is there our leaders fail us - they lag behind the hope and believe of the masses. I understand thoroughly that no one nation is going to put such a concept into effect until the others do so - at least until all the other great nations agree. They could, however, set the norm.

If the four or five stronger countries should do so, it would be impossible for anyone else to violate the code. Pass such a legislative fiat making it conditional upon the others doing so and you will thus take the moral leadership of the world.

Texas Legislature,
Austin, Texas,
June 13, 1951

The Alamo! On this hallowed soil at a crucial moment in history, a small band of Texans stood and died rather than yield the precious concept of liberty. The sacrifice they here and then made has inspired the hearts and steeled the arms of all succeeding generations and has become a mighty and noble part of the American tradition. It has influenced the course of all battles we have since fought and has contributed effectively to all victories we have since won. It is in its spirit that our nation has met and overcome the successive crises which have beset its progress. And it is in its spirit that we must meet the problems which now dominate human thought. The great issue of the day is whether we are departing from that spirit in the shaping of national policy to meet the challenge of the time. Are we failing it? Are we lacking the spiritual courage to adjudge issues upon the simple test of what seems right and what seems wrong? Are we content to compromise basic principle, to appease the savage instincts underlying ruthless aggression, to cower before the verbal whip-lash of an international bully? These are questions now agitating and disturbing the public conscience.

San Antonio, Texas,
June 15, 1951

...it is well that we understand that battles are not won by arms alone. There must exist above all else a spiritual impulse - a will to victory. This can only be if the soldier feels his sacrifice is to preserve the highest of moral values.

National Convention, The American Legion,
Miami, Florida,
October 17, 1951

...we find our western defense geared to an Island chain off the coast of continental Asia from which with air and sea supremacy we can dominate any predatory more threatening the Pacific Ocean area.

Opening, Centennial Celebration,
Seattle, Washington,
November 13, 1951

The potentiality of America's industrial strength in support of our expanding armament is guarantee against any wilfully designed military action against us. But wars can come about through blundering statesmanship animated by a lust for political power. Our course can and must be designed to promote the peace.

Opening, Centennial Celebration,
Seattle, Washington,
November 13, 1951

Possibly in Asia, where the record is more fully developed and events themselves have more plainly written the judgment, has the irresponsibility of our national policy been more pronounced. There our betrayal of China will ever stand as a black mark upon our escutcheon. But the tragedy of Korea comes closer to the hearts of the American people. For there thousands of our beloved dead give mute evidence to the tragic failure of American leadership.

Mississippi Legislature,
Jackson, Mississippi,
March 22, 1952

We defeated the northern Korean armies. But in the wake of the commitment of Communist China against us, we again repudiated our purpose to weld all of Korea into a free nation and denied our own beleaguered forces the orthodox military means which offered promise of early victory.

Mississippi Legislature,
Jackson, Mississippi,
March 22, 1952

(On Korea) We have permitted the enemy with impunity to prepare his blows against us from behind arbitrary and unreasonable sanctuary. We have protected him by holding inviolate his own soil, his war-making facilities and his own nearby bases of attack.

Mississippi Legislature,
Jackson, Mississippi,
March 22, 1952

...death has come to hundreds of thousands of defenseless Korean civilians and a nation brought under our sacred protection has been devastated and gutted. As long as history is written, the shame of this will be recorded, but its more immediate consequences will be found in the loss of the faith of Asia in our nation's pledged word and the consequent undermining of the foundations to the future peace of the world.

> *Mississippi Legislature,*
> *Jackson, Mississippi,*
> *March 22, 1952*

It is an unassailable truth that the science of industry has become a major element in the science of war.

> *National Association of Manufacturers,*
> *Waldorf-Astoria Hotel, New York, New York,*
> *December 5, 1952*

Never before has this Nation been engaged in mortal combat with a hostile power without military objective, without policy other than restrictions governing operations, or indeed without even formally recognizing a state of war. Wherever and whenever Americans foregather, this issue should be foremost in their deliberations and the question must be asked and repeated time and time again of those in authority and responsibility: "What do you intend to do about Korea?"

> *National Association of Manufacturers,*
> *Waldorf-Astoria Hotel, New York, New York,*
> *December 5, 1952*

Every nation that has what is valuable is obligated to be prepared to defend against brutal attack or unjust effort to seize and appropriate. ... Every nation that would preserve its tranquility, its riches, its independence, and its self-respect must keep alive its martial ardor and be at all time prepared to defend itself.

> *Veterans of the Rainbow (42nd) Infantry*
> *Division of World War I,*
> *Washington, DC,*
> *July 14, 1935*

In the last 3,400 years only 268 - less than 1 in 13 - have been free from wars. No wonder that Plato, the wisest of all men, once exclaimed, "Only the dead have seen the end of war."

> *Veterans of the Rainbow (42nd) Infantry*
> *Division of World War I,*
> *Washington, DC,*
> *July 14, 1935*

From the dawn of history to the present day it has always been the militant aggressor taking the place of the unprepared.

Veterans of the Rainbow (42nd) Infantry
Division of World War I,
Washington, DC,
July 14, 1935

Success in war depends upon men, not money. ... Indeed nothing is more insolent or provocative or more apt to lead to a breach of the peace than undefended riches among armed men.

Veterans of the Rainbow (42nd) Infantry
Division of World War I,
Washington, DC,
July 14, 1935

... was an example of the inflexibility in the pursuit of previously conceived ideas that is, unfortunately, too frequent in modern warfare. Final decisions are made not at the front by those who are there, but many miles away by those who can but guess at the possibilities and potentialities. The essence of victory lies in the answer to where and when.

General of the Army Douglas MacArthur
"Reminiscences"
McGraw-Hill Book Company, New York, 1964

This experience (Korea) - again emphasizes the utter futility of modern war...

Massachusetts Legislature,
Boston, Massachusetts,
July 25, 1951

Could anything be more agonizing to the mothers of their dead than the belittling reference to it by the Joint Chiefs of Staff as the "Korean Skirmish?"

National Convention, The American Legion,
Miami, Florida,
October 17, 1951

While we must be prepared to meet the trial of war if war comes, we should gear our foreign and domestic policies toward the ultimate goal - the abolition of war from the face of the earth.

Massachusetts Legislature,
Boston, Massachusetts,
July 25, 1951

Our ideal must be eventually the abolition of war.

Keynote Address,
Republic National Convention,
Chicago, Illinois,
July 7, 1952

No man in the world is more anxious to avoid the expansion of war than I. I am a one hundred per cent disbeliever in war. The enormous sacrifices that have been brought about by scientific methods of killing have rendered war a fantastic and impossible method for the solution of international difficulties.

Texas Legislature,
Austin, Texas,
June 13, 1951

I called for reinforcements, but was informed that reinforcements were not available. I made clear that if not permitted to destroy the enemy build-up bases north of the Yalu; if not permitted to utilize the friendly Chinese forces of some 600,000 men on Formosa; if not permitted to blockade the China coast to prevent the Chinese Reds from getting succor from without; and if there were to be no hope of major reinforcements, the position of the command from the military standpoint forbade victory.

U. S. Congress,
Washington, DC,
April 19, 1951

Recent events point to a startling and dangerous shift in our basic military concept. After Communist China committed itself to war against our forces in Korea, our political and military leaders set aside our traditional military policy calling for the employment of all available power and means to achieve a prompt and decisive victory and adopted instead the doctrine of defense.

Every distinguished military leader of the past and all military experience from the beginning of time warns this but invites failure.

Under this new conception, novel indeed to the American military character, we are required in the midst of deadly war to soften our blows and send men into battle with neither promise nor hope of victory. We have deprived them of supporting military power already on hand and available which would blunt the enemy's blows against them, save countless American lives, fulfill our commitment to the tragic people of Korea and lead to the victorious end of a war which has already left so many thousands of American soldiers maimed or dead.

More than this, it could and would have removed the Chinese Communists as a threat to freedom in Asia and the peace of the world for generations to come.

National Convention, The American Legion,
Miami, Florida,
October 17, 1951

In Korea, despite the magnificent performance of our fighting forces, the result has been indecisive. The high moral purpose which so animated and inspired the world a year ago yielded to the timidity and fear of our leaders as after defeating our original enemy a new one entered the field which they dared not fight to a decision.

Appeasement thereafter became the policy of war on the battlefield.

In the actual fighting with this new enemy we did not lose but neither did we win. Yet, it can be accepted as a basic principle proven and reproven since the beginning of time that a great nation which enters upon war and fails to see it through to victory must accept the full moral consequence of defeat.

Massachusetts Legislature,
Boston, Massachusetts,
July 25, 1951

I have believed a realistic policy should fill the long existing vacuum left in the wake of Red China's commitment to war against us - a policy designed to affect the early restoration of peace, through victory, with a consequent saving of countless American lives. It is difficult to ask men to fight and die unless we give them a realistic mission and means to accomplish it.

Chicago, Illinois,
April 26, 1951

If all other evidence were ignored, our mounting dead would alone stand as mute evidence that it is war in which we are now actually engaged. Yet, despite this, they seek to avoid the grave responsibility inherent in the fact of war; seek to divert public thought from the basic issue which war creates; how may victory be achieved with a minimum of human sacrifice. It is not a question of who wants war and who wants peace. All men of good conscience earnestly seek peace. The method alone is in issue. Some, with me, would achieve peace through a prompt and decisive victory at a saving of human life, others through appeasement and compromise of moral principle, with less regard for human life. The one course follows our great American tradition, the other but can lead to unending slaughter and our country's moral debasement.

Dallas, Texas,
June 15, 1951

There are some who for varying reasons would appease Red China. They are blind to history's clear lesson. For history teaches with unmistakable emphasis that appeasement but begets new and bloodier war. It points to no single instance where the end has justified that means - where appeasement has led to more than a sham peace. Like blackmail, it lays the basis for new and successively greater demands, until, as in blackmail, violence becomes the only other alternative.

"Why," my soldiers asked of me, "surrender military advantages to an enemy in the field?" I could not answer. Some may say to avoid spread of the conflict into an all-out war with China; others, to avoid Soviet intervention. Neither explanation seems valid. For China is already engaging with the maximum power it can commit and the Soviet will not necessarily mesh its actions with our moves. Like a cobra, any new enemy will more likely strike whenever it feels that the relativity in military or other potential is in its favor on a world-wide basis.

U. S. Congress,
Washington, DC,
April 19, 1951

We have been told of the war in Korea that it is the wrong war, with the wrong enemy, at the wrong time and in the wrong place. Does this mean that they intend and indeed plan what they would call a right war, wit a right enemy, at a right time and in the right place?

If successful in mounting the North Atlantic Pact in 1953 or 1954 or at one of the ever-changing dates fixed for its consummation, what comes then? Do we mean to throw down the gage of battle? Do we mean to continue the fantastic fiscal burden indefinitely to our inevitable exhaustion?

Massachusetts Legislature,
Boston, Massachusetts,
July 25, 1951

Munich, and many other historical examples, have taught us that diplomatic appeasement but sows the seeds of future conflict. Yet, oblivious to these bloody lessons, we now practice a new and yet more dangerous form of appeasement - appeasement on the battlefield where under we soften our blows, withhold our power, and surrender military advantages, in apparent hope that in some nebulous way by so doing a potential enemy will be coerced to desist from attacking us.

Texas Legislature,
Austin, Texas,
June 13, 1951

The greatest hazard under which we now labor is the fear that the policy and propaganda of our present leadership may be setting the stage for a third world war. We are following the same path - the same historical record - the same political concept and leadership - which projected us into World War I, World War II, and the war in Korea.

Since before the close of World War II, this leadership has contributed to the building of Soviet military strength by extravagant lend-lease aid quite beyond any common military need; by acquiescing in Soviet troop concentration and dispositions at highly strategic points in Europe and Asia; by abandoning our war-time allies to the pressure of Soviet conquest; and, at the same time, divesting ourselves of our own vastly superior military strength, with reckless and precipitate haste.

Against this background none will quarrel with the need to regain adequate security forces, not only that we may be prepared to meet any external threat, but that our diplomacy may be bulwarked with a power which will command universal respect.

But we cannot be satisfied with a leadership which declaims a devotion to peace with constant platitudinous statements and phrases while taking steps which inexorably tend to lead toward war.

Opening, Centennial Celebration,
Seattle, Washington,
November 13, 1951

You cannot control war; you can only abolish it. Those who shrug this off as idealistic are the real enemies of peace - the real war mongers. Those who lack the enterprise, vision and courage to try a new approach when none others have succeeded fail completely the most simple test of leadership.

Massachusetts Legislature,
Boston, Massachusetts,
July 25, 1951

MacArthur speaks to the 24th Infantry Division at Taranevah Bay, Hollandia, April 1944.

Let us regain some of the courage and faith of the architects who charted the course to our past greatness. Let us look up as befits the most powerful nation on earth, both spiritually and physically.

Let us tell all that while firmly and invincibly dedicated to the course of peace, we will not shrink from defending ourselves if the alternative is slavery or some other form of moral degradation.

Let us proudly reassume our traditional role of readiness to meet and vanquish the forces of evil at any time and any place they are hurled against us. Let us make clear our eagerness to abolish the scourge of war from the face of the earth just as soon as others are willing to rise to so noble a stature with us. Let us renew our reverence for the blood of our sons and strike with all the power we can mount to support and protect those who now fight our battles in distant lands.

And above all else let us regain our faith in ourselves and rededicate all that is within us to the repair and preservation of our own free institutions and the advance of our own free destiny.

> *Texas Legislature,*
> *Austin, Texas,*
> *June 13, 1951*

Various methods through the ages have attempted to devise an international process to prevent or settle disputes between nations. ...the mechanics ...have never been successful. ...leaving the only path to be by way of the crucible of war. The utter destructiveness of war now blots out this alternative.

> *VJ Day Broadcast, U.S.S. Missouri,*
> *Tokyo Bay,*
> *September 2, 1945*

The problem basically is theological and involves a spiritual recrudescence... It must be of the spirit if we are to save the flesh.

> *VJ Day Broadcast, U.S.S. Missouri,*
> *Tokyo Bay,*
> *September 2, 1945*

Preparedness is the key to success and victory.

> *General of the Army Douglas MacArthur*
> *"Reminiscences"*
> *McGraw-Hill Book Company, New York, 1964*

The taste of freedom is a heady wine that ultimately no human being can resist.

> *General of the Army Douglas MacArthur*
> *"Reminiscences"*
> *McGraw-Hill Book Company, New York, 1964*

No military problem is unsolvable. Korea stands today as the hallowed grave-yard for countless American dead. We must not let it become as well a grave-yard for American hope, American faith, and American honor.

Keynote Address,
Republican National Convention,
Chicago, Illinois,
July 7, 1952

The days of the frontal attack should be over. Modern infantry weapons are too deadly and frontal assault is only for mediocre commanders. Good com-manders do not turn in heavy losses.

General of the Army Douglas MacArthur
"Reminiscences"
McGraw-Hill Book Company, New York, 1964

For years I have believed that war should be abolished as an outmoded means of resolving disputes between nations. Probably no living man has seen as much of war and its destruction as I had. A participant or observer in six wars, a vet-eran of twenty campaigns, the survivor of hundreds of battlefields, I have fought with or against the soldiers of practically every country in the world, and my abhorrence reached its height with the perfection of the atom bomb.

General of the Army Douglas MacArthur
"Reminiscences"
McGraw-Hill Book Company, New York, 1964

Editor's note: The Appropriations committee of the U. S. House of Represen-tatives wanted to know how MacArthur could justify the expenditure of Army appropriations to feed the just conquered Japanese. Excerpt from his letter fol-lows:

...starvation breeds mass unrest, disorder and violence. Give me bread or give me bullets.

General of the Army Douglas MacArthur
"Reminiscences"
McGraw-Hill Book Company, New York, 1964

Surprise is the most vital element for success in war.

General of the Army Douglas MacArthur
"Reminiscences"
McGraw-Hill Book Company, New York, 1964

New conditions and new weapons require new and imaginative methods for solution and application. Wars are never won in the past.

General of the Army Douglas MacArthur
"Reminiscences"
McGraw-Hill Book Company, New York, 1964

The coming battle (Leyte invasion) was to demonstrate the dangers involved in the lack of unified command and the misunderstandings that can ensue during major operations in which the commander ultimately responsible does not have full control over all forces in the operation.

General of the Army Douglas MacArthur
"Reminiscences"
McGraw-Hill Book Company, New York, 1964

Indeed, the greatest satisfaction I have always felt as a result of campaign successes is of the men I saved and brought back safely rather than the glory of the victories that were gained.

General of the Army Douglas MacArthur
"Reminiscences"
McGraw-Hill Book Company, New York, 1964

...as I prepared to receive the surrender of the mighty warlords of the Far East, I wish that my pen were wielded by one on such intimate terms with words - those immortal heralds of thought which at the touch of genius become radiant - that at my call they would convey my feelings in terms that would satisfy the ultimate sources of reason, history and interpretation. For I have a consciousness that in the events culminating at this immortal moment lie those truths which at last are transplanted into epics and lyrics, and those exalted terms which we find on the lips of the great seers and prophets.

General of the Army Douglas MacArthur
"Reminiscences"
McGraw-Hill Book Company, New York, 1964

A great nation which enters upon war and does not see it through to victory will ultimately suffer all the consequences of defeat. Stalemate may end the casualties on the battlefield, but marks the military collapse of the purpose which induced entry into combat.

General of the Army Douglas MacArthur
"Reminiscences"
McGraw-Hill Book Company, New York, 1964

...the sacrifice leading to a military victory would be pointless did we not translate it promptly to the political advantage of peace.

General of the Army Douglas MacArthur
"Reminiscences"
McGraw-Hill Book Company, New York, 1964

Editor's note: Statement made by MacArthur during an August 23, 1950 strategic conference to debate a possible amphibious landing in Korea.
The bulk of the Reds are committed around Walker's defense perimeter. The enemy, I am convinced, has failed to prepare Inchon properly for defense. The very arguments you have made as to the impracticabilities involved will tend to ensure for me the element of surprise. For the enemy commander will reason that no one would be so brash as to make such an attempt. Surprise is the most

vital element for success in war. ...the North Koreans would regard an Inchon landing as impossible. ...I could take them by surprise.

The Navy's objections... are indeed substantial and pertinent. But they are not insuperable. My confidence in the navy is complete...

As to the proposal for a landing at Kunsan, it would indeed eliminate many of the hazards of Inchon, but it would be largely ineffective and indecisive. It would be an attempted envelopment which would not envelop. It would not sever or destroy the enemy's supply lines or distribution center, and would therefore serve little purpose. It would be a "short envelopment," and nothing in war is more futile. Better no flank movement than one such as this. ...

But seizure of Inchon and Seoul will cut the enemy's supply line and seal off the entire southern peninsula. The vulnerability of the enemy is his supply position. ... By seizing Seoul I would completely paralyze the enemy's supply system - coming and going. This in turn will paralyze the fighting power of the troops ... Without munitions and food they will soon be helpless and disorganized, and can easily be overpowered by our smaller but well-supplied forces.

The only alternative to a stroke such as I propose will be the continuation of the savage sacrifice we are making at Pusan, with no hope of relief in sight. Are you content to let our troops stay in that bloody perimeter like beef cattle in the slaughterhouse? Who will take the responsibility for such a tragedy? Certainly, I will not.

The prestige of the Western world hangs in the balance. Oriental millions are watching the outcome. ... If we lose the war to Communism in Asia, the fate of Europe will be gravely jeopardized. Win it and Europe will probably be saved from war and stay free. Make the wrong decision here - the fatal decision of inertia - and we will be done. I can almost hear the ticking of the second hand of destiny. We must act now or we will die.

If my estimate is inaccurate and should I run into a defense with which I cannot cope, I will be there personally and will immediately withdraw our forces before they are committed to a bloody setback. The only loss then will be my professional reputation. But Inchon will not fail. Inchon will succeed. And it will save 100,000 lives.

General of the Army Douglas MacArthur
"Reminiscences"
McGraw-Hill Book Company, New York, 1964

Editor's note: The following statements from the book "MacArthur His Rendevous with History" by Maj. Gen. Cornelius Whitney, Alfred A. Knopf, New York, 1956, were thought to be significant and therefore included:

MacArthur's military philosophy was well defined. Although he perceived a direct relationship between politics and war, he did not accept the Clausewitzian theory of war as a mere continuation of politics. He believed instead:

"The whole purpose of combat and war is to create a situation in which victory on the battlefield can be promptly translated into a politically advantageous peace. Success in war involves political exploitation as well as military victory. The sacrifices leading to a military victory would be pointless if not translated promptly into the political advantages of peace."

MacArthur believed that once a nation went to war, it should concert all effort toward winning that war as quickly as possible. He rejected the concept of defensive warfare. When Clare Boothe asked him what his formula for defensive warfare was, he tersely answered, "Defeat." He pointed out that "in no other profession are the penalties for employing untrained personnel so appalling and so irrevocable as in the military."

AFTER WORD

Editors note: MacArthur's ability to manage manpower, material and all resources can be summed up by these final comments to this work. The list also reflects about everything you should know about the man.

DOUGLAS MACARTHUR'S PRINCIPLES OF LEADERSHIP

Do I heckle my subordinates or strengthen and encourage them?

Do I use moral courage in getting rid of subordinates who have proven themselves beyond doubt to be unfit?

Have I done all in my power by encouragement, incentive and spur to salvage the weak and erring?

Do I know by NAME and CHARACTER a maximum number of subordinates for whom I am responsible? Do I know them intimately?

Am I thoroughly familiar with the technique, necessities, objectives and administration of my job?

Do I lose my temper at individuals?

Do I act in such a way as to make my subordinates WANT to follow me?

Do I delegate tasks which should be mine?

Do I arrogate everything to myself and delegate nothing?

Do I develop my subordinates by placing on each one as much responsibility as he can stand?

Am I interested in the personal welfare of each of my subordinates, as if he were a member of my family?

Have I the calmness of voice and manner to inspire confidence, or am I inclined to irascibility and excitability?

Am I a constant example to my subordinates in character, dress, deportment and courtesy?

Am I inclined to be nice to my superiors and mean to my subordinates?

Is my door open to my subordinates?

Do I think more of POSITION than JOB?

Do I correct a subordinate in front of others?

APPENDIX

"A Father's Prayer"

Build me a son, O Lord, who will be strong enough to know when he is weak, and brave enough to face himself when he is afraid; one who will be proud and unbending in honest defeat, and humble and gentle in victory.

Build me a son whose wishes will not take the place of deeds; a son who will know Thee - and that to know himself is the foundation stone of knowledge.

Lead him, I pray, not in the path of ease and comfort, but under the stress and spur of difficulties and challenge. Here let him learn to stand up in the storm; here let him learn compassion for those who fail.

Build me a son whose heart will be clear, whose goal will be high; a son who will master himself before he seeks to master other men; one who will reach into the future, yet never forget the past.

And after all these things are his, add, I pray, enough of a sense of humor, so that he may always be serious, yet never take himself too seriously. Give him humility, so that he may always remember the simplicity of true greatness, the open mind of true wisdom, and the meekness of true strength.

Then, I, his father, will dare to whisper, "I have not lived in vain."

MacArthur with his wife and son at the dedication of a park in his mother's name, November 1951.

BIBLIOGRAPHY

John M. Pratt, Editor
Revitalizing a Nation: A Statement of Beliefs, Opinions & Policies Embodied in the Public Pronouncements of General of the Army Douglas MacArthur
©1952, Chicago: The Heritage Foundation, Inc., Heritage Press

Major Vorin E. Whan, Jr., USA, Editor
A Soldier Speaks
Public Papers and Speeches of General of the Army Douglas MacArthur
©1965 Frederick A. Praeger, Publishers, New York, NY

Frank C. Waldrop, Editor
MacArthur On War
Duell, Sloan and Pearce, New York
©1942 by Frank C. Waldrop

U.S. Senate, 88th Congress, 2nd Session, Document No. 95
Compiled by the Legislative Reference Service, Library of Congress
Representative Speeches of General of the Army Douglas MacArthur
April 29, 1964 - Ordered to be printed
U.S. Government Printing Office, Washington: 1964

Audio Tape
World War II - Six speeches delivered during World War II
Produced by: General Douglas MacArthur Foundation

Audio Tape
Sentimental Journey - Five speeches delivered during return to the Philippines, July 3-12, 1961
Produced by: General Douglas MacArthur Foundation

Armel Dyer
The Oratory of Douglas MacArthur
Dissertation, University of Oregon, Ph.D., 1968
©1968 by Armel Dyer

General George C. Kenney
The MacArthur I Know
Duell, Sloan and Pearce, New York, ©1951

General of the Army Douglas MacArthur
Reminiscences
McGraw-Hill Book Company, New York, 1964,©1964 by Time, Inc.

Major General Courtney Whitney
MacArthur: His Rendezvous With History
Alfred A. Knopf, New York, 1956, © Time, Inc., 1955

James W. Zobel
Archivist, General Douglas MacArthur Foundation
Norfolk, Virginia

Historian
United States Military Academy
West Point, New York

ABOUT THE AUTHOR

Colonel Edward T. Imparato, a member of a family of eight siblings, was born in Flushing, New York. The family moved to Saugerties, New York, 100 miles north of New York City on the shore of the beautiful Hudson River. His early and strong desire was to be a flyer. From age six to graduation from high school the passion for flying seemed to increase by the year. The day after graduation he departed his home town to enroll at the Ryan School of Aeronautics. After graduating from Ryan with honors and a license as a Master Aircraft and Engine Mechanic and a Commercial Pilot, he opened his own flying school at Lemon Grove at San Diego, California.

Joining the U.S. Army Air Corp unit at Lindbergh Field in order to fly bigger and faster aircraft, he was called to active duty with the Army Air Force in November 1938, transferring to Randolph and Kelly Field - the West Point of the Air.

War clouds were on the horizon and one week after the war with Japan was declared, he received transfer orders to Australia in order to organize a transport squadron to provide airborne support for the Army ground troops in the South West Pacific.

After serving 40 months with General Douglas MacArthur, Imparato was assigned to stateside duty.

Shortly thereafter he was ordered to the Army's Command and General Staff College at Ft. Leavenworth, Kansas. Later attended a Senior Management course at George Washington University, Washington, D.C. Upon graduation from the Air War college he was transferred to Germany with his unit to participate in the Berlin Air Lift. Further duty took him to Panama as Chief of Staff of the Carribean Air Command and Inspector of all MAAG units in the countries of Central and South America. In 1995 he was assigned to the Air War College.

He retired from the Air Force as a Full Colonel in June 1961. Writing and publishing histories of World War II in the Pacific, he has produced seven books and is still writing.